Haunted Vending Machine

(A collection of ghost stories.)

Remedy Hawke

This book is dedicated to two special ladies who encouraged me by saying, "You should write a book."

Their names are Cathy J. Quawpaw and Cece Perez. Thank you for believing in me. Contact me, ladies, for your free copy.

And of course to all others who helped me on this project in their various ways.

And to Jade, your loyalty to your family is remarkable.

And to Michael for being so stalwart.

And for all who are reading this book:

May God bless and keep you, and hold your hand when you need it through difficult spots in life. May his countenance smile upon you and prosper you along the way. May you have joy and peace and be able to bestow this on others around you. May you be an example of how to live and how to fulfill. May others who copy you find their special assignment serendipitously so that they can be fulfilled as well. And may you fix yourself so that the world will be fixed.

Love and blessings,

Remedy Hawke

Let me just give you a heads up here:

I named this book Haunted Vending Machine, because I'm not going to assign chapters to these stories. Select and read as you would a snack from a vending machine.

I am going to share my ghost and cryptid encounters in here because 'tis the season for spooky and chills and thought provoking encounters. Maybe a few tales involving my extra sensory skills.

Autumn (and even Halloween) is a time where we reflect on our lives each year. It's an uncanny thing I've noticed and a strong part of human nature.

But you should also expect to read them again in my autobiography. They are my stories after all. I am the one who experienced them.

You might not find them all in there or all in here because I'm human and I might forget one when compiling the other book, or suddenly remember one I forgot to include in this one.

My purpose in putting this conversation piece together is to stimulate your minds and allow you to find enjoyment in these true tales.

I'd also like to point out that in THOUSANDS OF YEARS ON THIS PLANET, psychics are still being doubted and ridiculed. And yet there continues to be ghost and cryptid sightings, people who can see into the future, others who can know things without knowing them before, people with the gift of sight, taste, smell, touch, hearing and a few other extras. Some of them have better ethics than others, just like in any profession or group. Some of them charge for their services, others do not. And some are better at it than others.

In the bible and the Torah, a psychic is known as a Sage or a Prophet, and there are Prophetesses and female sages as well.

In fact, most of us are psychic whether we realize it or not.

I hope you enjoy this book.

Contents

Otherwhere & Otherwhen 9

Dragonflies 13

9 11 2001 16

All Star Motel 22

12 Inches Of Ash 25

13 Repeats 29

A Visit From The Patriarch 32

Bigfoot or Bopawee? 35

Chanting the Gohonzon 38

Cousin Kae In The Storehouse Of Souls 40

Dr. Erin Stone 45

Eye Of The Tornado 49

Fire In The Night 52

Ghost Dwarf of Tahquitz Canyon 57

Ghostly Warning 59

Grandma Carole 62

Grandma Leona's China Hutch 64

Green Monsters 68

Haunted Trucking School 70

The Time I Was Mistaken As A Ghost 72

Kitchen Spirits and Tea 82

Lightning Fingers 84

Ma Belle, Yisraelle 86

Maybe He Just Needs Love – NOPE!! 89

My Bird Died 93

My First Of Many Nirvana Experiences. 94

My Friend Goh-tu..97

My Grandma Helen Looks Out For Me 102

Peeping-Tom Artist 105

Pneumonaultramicroscopicsilicavolcanoconiosis 106

Safeway Ghost 108

Snowmist Warriors 112

That Place Is Unclean 114

The Dark Mass Of Energy.......................................119

The Devil Dog 122

The Ghost At The Hot Springs Pools 125

The Ghosts Of C.A.P.S. 127

The Kind Yunweh Tsunsdi 133

The Nice Mother-in-law 135

The Stairs on State Street 139

The Three Ghosts of Green Street 142

The Yellow Ski Mask..145

There's A Reason They Call It Water Street 148

Otherwhere & Otherwhen

Let me just start this book with the notion that I was a ghost to begin with. Or, rather, a spirit. Just like most of us. At this point in the game, most of us have lived a previous life or many previous lives.

The odd thing about this one for me is that I remember a little bit of before, in the Otherwhere/Otherwhen. What most people call the Spirit World. I call it this because it is here, but not here. And it is now, but not now. Hence, Otherwhere and Otherwhen. The side of that token I utilize most is Otherwhere. Not sure why.

I remember I was doing something with a mountain. The most specific I can get with this is to say that my arms were reaching into it to fix something. I don't know what.

I got interrupted by a messenger coming and telling me that I was needed and would be going in to help with things.

I remember that I was wearing something with tippetted sleeves and very flowy. And long. My hair was long.

I followed this messenger to a place that was sort of like a cave, and stood and waited.

Then I was suddenly riding inside some kind of capsule and dropping in a spiral. I knew I had done this several times and I said aloud, "I hate this!"

There was someone riding in a capsule next to me that had a long squiggly thing on top. I could only see his face and that he was male when he would look directly at me through this capsule.

He smiled at me and then laughed as we bounced and spun together down this dark tunnel. "Why don't you like this? It's fun! And sometimes you go inside the snowball there and snuggle in and have a nice life."

I looked ahead and saw a large glowing white ball. The energy emitted from it in little patches of sunbeam yellow. It seemed to have spikes, but when my capsule seemed it was going to crash into it, it slowed down and it seemed I was moving through a glowing white cloud.

I saw a story, starring me, playing very quickly on the screens in front of me. There seemed to be three of these screens. Sometimes I could choose one of the screens and sometimes they were all the same. No choice.

I heard a male voice say something, but didn't understand what was meant by what he said. Something like "This is your life. You must choose how you will build it."

I asked the voice what was happening there.

I said something like, "I need to find out where I am first."

The images stopped playing, the screens disappeared, and I felt myself curling up as though I were in a warm blanket snuggled up.

Every once in a while I'll feel an overwhelming sleepiness and find myself curling up like this in an actual blanket. I see a precognitive movie of the next phase of my life and try to decipher what is happening. While I'm typing this, I suddenly realize that the next time this happens I need to DECIDE what is happening. This is making me laugh at myself right now.

I kept having this dream, sometimes in more detail, sometimes it would just be the spinning in the tunnel or corridor and then cut off because I would wake up terrified.

I don't know why I would then feel like going to look at a little book my adoptive mom had bought named "You Were Smaller Than A Dot" by RN Glen C. Griffin and Mary Ella Griffin. But I would almost immediately go find it. I'd read it, look at the pictures, and then put it back. Like I was trying to figure out what it was that was calling to me in that book.

This went on until I was married and in my 20s, and on my 3rd pregnancy, when suddenly I realized what this bizarre memory was that sometimes presented as a flashback, and sometimes as a nightmare.

It happened while I was looking at book on pregnancy and birth I had bought myself to understand the process better. And while I was looking at a sketch of a sperm, tail up, like the capsule that other person was riding in next to mine.

We were being ejaculated into my mother and I was the one that impregnated the egg.

I was very surprised.

I suddenly realized how real everything was on both sides of the invisible barrier that separates the Otherwhere & Otherwhen from each other. And that reality here is meant to be different from reality there, but it is no less real on either side.

Each of these sides has a purpose.

We slide back and forth like a fluid in osmosis until we reach our best mix of attributes and talents and skills. Until we become our best self.

And while we are here, we are supposed to focus on what we are doing here, and never mind about the Otherwhere & Otherwhen.

I hope that this piece of my paradigm can help each of you to realize how beautiful you are inside. And not in the way that we see each other's faces and bodies. But beautiful like a star. Glowing and sparking and filled with potential.

I hope that you will understand that just as many wise Eastern philosophers have mentioned in various ways, the only way to win is to be in competition with yourself. To focus on yourself.

And the only way to fix the world is to start with yourself. With the person in the mirror that you see when you're in the bathroom.

If you get irritated with your own face when you look at yourself, it's not because of how you look. It is yourself trying to remember what it was you were supposed to do that you didn't. And sometimes it's yourself reminding yourself to make something right. Something that you broke, or a person you hurt or stole from. Or snubbed. To give credit where credit is due. Or to tell the truth regarding someone you lied about. To finally keep a promise. You are never going to like your own face no matter how much plastic surgery you get, the haircut you switch to, or the makeup you wear until you know that you can navigate amongst humanity with a clear conscience.

I know, because I've experienced this phasing many times in this life.

I own several self-improvement books because I know that you can always do with an upgrade. All of us can.

Until you die, you can always add one more level up in your spiritual or mental abilities and knowledge.

I can honestly say that I like myself now.

I cannot honestly say that I am finished improving myself.

The day this happens I will be finished coming back here. Except maybe to check on those of you I left behind, and help you if I can.

Ask my classmates at Ç R England Trucking School if I stayed back to help them figure out the trick of climbing into and out of a semi-trailer when you're short.

This is who I am. I want us all to win. I want us all to succeed.

Dragonflies

I have developed a strong affection for dragonflies, every color of them. And there are quite a few different colors. There are in Virginia, where all of my children were born, anyway.

So while living on Elektra Drive in Newport News, which was still airport property in 2000, there were some difficulties with the lot we were on.

For whatever reason, there were deep ditches dug at each of the corners and storm drains installed, but these ditches didn't go all the way around the block, not even as gutters! So every time the rainy season came, not only did the hibernating frogs suddenly take over the neighborhood, but your yard became a muddy, swampy mess.

I was not having this, and I went and bought a shovel so I could make gutters at least for the rain to run off of my lawn. A lawn I had painstakingly grown from seed from the little 2 x 2 patch I had when I moved in. And I had to do this because the former tenants had worked on their cars right up in the yard next to the house and killed the grass with their used oil and such.

This greatly diminished the amount of mosquitoes and flies hovering around my door, to my pleasant surprise. And this was the first year people were talking about West Nile Virus. Top that off with the benefit of dozens of dragonflies appearing in our yard after our trips to the lake near Christopher Newport University, where fishing was free and dragonflies lived in massive flocks, and I never got bit by a single mosquito again, nor did I have any flies in my house after this. The kids and I used to joke that maybe they followed us home from the lake after we fed them. Maybe they weren't wrong.

I love the way these sentient insects flirt with you with their honeycomb eye-bulbs and tilt their heads at you inquisitively, just like a family dog would. The fact that they will flutter onto your picnic table and try to interact with you, waiting for a crumb of bread, potato chip or tiny piece of hotdog or cheese tells me everything I need to know about whether they are sentient or not. And they are. Very.

And they became very pretty allies when I had yet another run in with my evil neighbor next door on my left.

This bitter woman had refused to let me continue the little gutter I'd made in front of my house past her front lawn. She told me, "I like my lawn." Even when I guaranteed I would do all the digging she refused.

So the rain came again and it was a gusher. Her lawn flooded, my lawn was just right. Even if my gutter was full because of the dam at the property line.

Wouldn't you know it, that bitch called the Health Department about my "standing water" and the potential for West Nile Virus because of mosquitoes.

I came home one afternoon and found a guy there with a clipboard. He was gazing around my yard, which now had nearly a full lawn, and flowers. And also gold, brown, black, red, dark green, light green, turquoise, navy blue, white, yellow and orange dragonflies (and I might have forgotten some colors) zipping about eating the mosquitoes and flies, and birds eating them, and little frogs by my gutter next to a school of tadpoles darting in and out of some moss that was overhanging the gutter.

He actually commented on the family of wolf spiders building a little twig bridge together across the gutter, as though it was a little tiny river they needed to cross.

I told him this was one of my family's favorite things, and that they have to rebuild it every time it rains.

He sighs and shrugs and says, "Your neighbor filed a complaint with us, but I'm looking at a miniature eco-system here. And I don't see a single mosquito that doesn't get eaten immediately by a dragonfly or a bird. It's amazing."

I smiled and realized how efficient the animals system had become in my yard. And then I thanked God silently for helping me.

"I'm unfounding this." He tore off my copy after writing UNFOUNDED in big red letters with his sharpie across it diagonally. "If you don't mind, could you share with me how you did this?"

He enjoyed my little scenarios about growing the grass and digging the ditch. "Amazing. I love this. You know, some people just worry too much. I'm going to go over there and tell her and give her copy to her."

Well, she wasn't home at the moment, but I didn't mention it and just finished bringing my groceries inside. And on one of my subsequent trips to the car, I hear swearing and look up to see a huge swarm of mosquitoes has engulfed him midway across her swampy lawn. I was dumbfounded. And delighted.

I tried not to laugh as he angrily swatted at these nuisance insects, and then flipped to a fresh form on his clipboard and wrote HER up for standing water. Hilarious!

He got to the street and looked at me as he exclaimed, "That…………WOMAN!"

"I know, I saw," I replied.

"Well I wrote *her* up!" He exclaimed.

"I'm sorry," I murmured.

"It's certainly not your fault. And again, I love what you've done here."

"Thanks!" I waved and smiled back as he waved and smiled and drove off. It felt really good to have someone acknowledge the good work I do for a change.

I hope he didn't contract West Nile virus, or whipworm from a pregnant mosquito. I suspect he was fine though.

And that is the story of how I came to love dragonflies, and probably the best gift God had given me up to that point.

9 11 2001

This was quite a shock for me. Well, duh. It was for pretty much all of us, wasn't it?

I was at Chris G's house using his internet to job hunt when the planes hit the towers. Specifically on the MSN home page before looking into a specific position I was after. The top story was, of course, the first plane in the tower. I thought at first it was an ad for a movie, maybe the next Die Hard? Then I thought it was someone's sick joke story, some exaggeration by The Onion maybe.

I couldn't yet fathom that kind of thing happening anywhere in the world at the moment because in the short time period between July 2001 and September of the same year, there seemed to be a happy lull in anything negative. I thought we were on the upswing globally and people were going to gradually begin to treat each other better. But looking back, I think I was just absorbed by my own problems and wasn't noticing anything else.

I pointed to the computer screen as Chris sat there watching something, can't remember what. "Look at what some twisted person thinks is funny, Chris."

He looked over at what I had in front of me and opened his mouth to say something, but stopped for a second. "Wait, I don't think that's a meme. Is that the MSN homepage?"

"Oh, yeah. The link I clicked in my email took me here. I was getting ready to go down my list of job links. I didn't notice the MSN logo until you pointed it out."

"I think that's real news, " he answered. "Let's check CNN." He pointed the remote at the t.v.

While we were listening to the newscasters talk about the first impact, the second occurred. It reminded me of those little frames will all the nails in them that you can press your face or hand into and it creates the shape on the other side. I don't care what the conspiracy theorists say about that one, I saw the nose and wings press the building, smoke and fire outward just like those nail frames. I can never forget that. It was cool and horrifying at the same time.

He kept watching the news reports on it, both of us not knowing that the towers would collapse soon.

I went into a chat room and began asking questions of others. There were responses from several military personnel who were off duty and began talking about getting called in for emergency assignment, which alarmed me. Some of what they were sharing could be strategically important if this turned into something more.

I was done wrapping up, submitted a few applications, and then told Chris I was freaking out inside the minute the Pentagon got hit.

"Well, everybody is," he replied.

"No, I mean....we live on airport property, my kids are in school except the little guy here, and I don't know if it's better to go pull them out of school and bring them here, or if this is actually not a safe place with the runways at the other end there."

He tilted his head and frowned. "Right?"

"Yes!"

The South Tower collapsed, (which confused me because it was hit second) and there was a flurry of intense discussion in the chat.

I began counseling these folks to watch what they were sharing on the internet because they had no way of knowing who was who. I got an immediate agreement from literally each one of them in the chat. I said, "Hey, pass it on to every service member you know and have them pass it along to the next, etc." Compliance. Agreement. It was like it was part of their boot camp training and such. I was so proud of them, and of their trainers. Wow.

And then the fourth plane pancaked into the ground in Pennsylvania.

And hey, I'm not anybody important – except that I am a US Citizen and that means something here more than anywhere else. We the People *are* the Government. That is what a Constitutional Republic is. The Constitution states firmly what the rules are and what the rights of the people are. And the word Republic actually means "rule by the people". Literally. We are our own governors. We are in an elite club of citizens who own their own fate. We should NEVER relinquish that. As I type there are conspirators who are engineering an invasion, have sold our ammo plants to a Czech billionaire under the guise of supplying Ukraine with ammo – but that whole battle between Russia and Ukraine is a ruse to make us unaware of the imminent invasion into Alaska. We need to posse up, folks.

But back to the September 11th situation as I experienced it that day....

Feeling as though I had talked to as many service members as I could, scanning for someone telling too much and then reminding them where we all were in there, I was wrapping things up with a female navy member, when Chris asked what I was doing. So I told him. I didn't realize he'd been watching me more than the news for several minutes – brought on by my rapid typing.

And then the 2nd tower fell. People were grieving now in that chat room. Everyone seemed to have someone in one of those buildings.

He got on the landline in his kitchen and was talking to someone who wasn't one of his usual friends or his sister. I don't remember the name he spoke. I was focused on this last chat when I overheard him say to this guy, "I think we should meet up. I'm noticing some very interesting behavior from my lady friend."

That got my attention. I asked him what he meant by that, and he said to not worry about it, just keep doing what I was doing.

0.o

 "Okay, that's it. I'm going home to pray and figure out what I need to do. See ya' Chris!" I shouted as I carried my things and Mickey out the door.

I was unaware that building 7 had collapsed as well until several days later. I was so caught up in my worry. I paced the entire length of my house for two hours while Mickey took his nap, fully prepared to scoop him up and go get the kids should the answer to my prayer be "Get a move on!" Or something similar. I could feel the sweat prickling my armpits the whole time. And I feel like when a person is this anxious they have a harder time getting the answer that God is trying to convey.

I read Torah, I prayed pretty much continuously, I cleaned like crazy and paced. Finally the kids came home.

Every time I looked at news videos on this or watched an actual broadcast, I noticed something weird. The billowing smoke they showed from the towers seemed to be shaped like different people that might be inside dying from the fire – but super huge. It was uncanny. I pointed this out to Chris the next time I was over there at his house. He agreed with me but didn't have much to share on it.

Along with my worry that something might happen to our neighborhood because of our proximity to the airport, and the fact that the airport owned the land we were sitting on, some other strange things happened to me and my family.

I got a birthday card from a muslim guy I met through a dating service who I had broken up with that contained cutaneous anthrax. It caused S-shaped scabs on the boils that formed on the left side of my face after barely tapping it, sniffing it (it smelled oddly of sandalwood but looked like used coffee grounds) and then running the two first fingers on my left hand down my cheek absentmindedly while reading what Ron Mahdi Thomas had written on the inside of the card. It was baffling how he acted as though I hadn't sent him packing 7 times in a row, with the threat of the police getting called if he ever showed up again. This is no exaggeration. This guy was not respecting my wishes not to date anymore.

When these boils developed under my skin, I didn't at first remember what had contacted my face in order to do that. Until I saw a local news story of the Jefferson Lab getting hit with an anthrax package, and they lied and said that no one was injured by it. When I remembered I went to the Health Department, who told me it wasn't Anthrax, but I should continue to take all of my Cipro. (Right.)

I know this because my daughter and her class had been on a one week workshop there from her magnet school and the facility decided it would be better if the families met in the school cafeteria for the family night to see what our kids had learned. While we were going to all the different booths, I saw the director talking to one of the police they had there for security, and as I walked up he saw my face, looked at her face and neck, and bowed out and walked over to talk to his R.O. (I think?) They were definitely discussing us from the glances and hand gestures.

I said, "You got anthraxed too, didn't you?"

She quickly said, "Shhhhhh!"

"Why are we keeping this quiet?" I queried.

"We don't want a panic."

"Do I look like I'm panicking?"

"No, but not everyone will be so stalwart."

I sighed and thanked her for teaching my daughter cool things, and then walked from the center of the cafeteria where she was over to the next booth.

Several other incidents occurred which culminated in me deciding the universe was telling me it was unsafe for me and my family in Virginia, and moving was definitely necessary. The rest of these stories are held in my memoirs.

I prayed and prayed about where to take my family in order to be safe, and was told to go to Los Angeles. This was odd to me, because I wasn't enjoying the career I had meant to yet. It felt like nothing for rent was affordable in LA. A friend at temple told me that perhaps I didn't need to be actually in LA, but in the vicinity. I thought that sounded like wise counsel so I set my target south of LA.

I ended up detouring to Utah thanks to the need I still had for acceptance from my imposter parents, as you can read about in the piece entitled "All Star Motel".

And there was no end of adventures and spooky encounters along the way during this move. I wasn't going to include this tale in this book, and make you wait for the autobiography, but the page in my notes where I had flipped to and bent it open backwards to was physically changed to this story when I woke up. I think I have a ghostly companion while I'm typing this book up for all of you. It's not a coincidence at all that 20 pages were flipped back and the notebook folded in half like that.

No one can deny, I guess, that there are more than 2,000 ghosts involved with the September 11ᵗʰ story. Where were you when this occurred? Were you safe? Did you have to flee? Did you lose loved ones?

I myself had been applying for a job with a law firm in one of those towers that July. I interviewed twice, and had a very good feeling about both interviews. When I was informed they wouldn't be flying me up there to interview in person because someone local had been selected, I was so furious I had yelled up at the ceiling to God about it asking him how I was supposed to take care of my children financially with these skimpy jobs in the town I was living in.

It wasn't until I moved to Colorado and accepted an invite to come to a service observing the anniversary of this tragedy, that I suddenly remembered how I had been protected from dying in that mess. Simply by not being selected for the job. It was 2011.

Let me tell you from the heart, sometimes God says no to keep you safe.

All Star Motel

I let myself take a one-year detour to Utah before escaping Virginia to California.

My imposter parents pleaded with me to let them help me. They claimed that because they had several single mothers for clients at their Montessori preschool they were able to understand how hard it was.

I shouldn't have believed them. I knew better having grown up in their household. And sure enough, they lived up to their reputation.

Instead of letting us come stay at their house like they'd promised over the phone, un-dad put us up in the All Star Motel in downtown Salt Lake City. They brought cheap $1 burgers and were not happy that Mickey looked Hispanic. (So that's what that look was that they gave me all the time. I always thought it was because I had done something wrong and walked around feeling guilty all the time.) Mickey was even darker than I had been at that age. It made me instinctively grit my teeth. Right out of the gate they had already broken their promises and were exhibiting the same behaviors they always had.

That night I cried a river. God had told me to go to California and here I had let these horrible excuses for parents talk me into trouble again. Like they had done when I tried to back out of my first marriage on my wedding night (the gypsy wedding that I was drugged into oblivion for doesn't count).

I begged God to understand my need for a family that cares about me. I told him I'm grateful for my kids, but I also need devoted parents, cousins, grandparents. Like I thought I had because they always told me I did, until I made a mistake or chose something they didn't agree with. Then it had always been a different story.

My real mother had died a year before I found out she was right down the road from me in Virginia. And my siblings by her had rejected me by walking out of the chapel at Saints Connie and Helen instead of coming to the multi-purpose building for coffee hour so we could talk. My step-father never acknowledged my voicemail, but he had heard a traffic case of mine – which I won pro se.

Laying there that night I was heartbroken. And even now it still stings like a thousand skewers to my chest.

Because I had divorced Fred, un-dad had told the rest of the family I was cut off. No one but my adoptive grandparents would talk to me out of 50+ people because of that. All of them I had formerly had what I thought were excellent and warm familial relationships with. And just like that, with a word from un-dad --- gone.

The lie of a supportive adoptive family was wounding.

And my ex-in-laws had never made me feel like I was part of their family. When I sent pictures of me and the kids to Norma, she would always call to chew me out and complain because only the grandkids could be on her wall. And that was before the divorce.

And here I lay in the worst motel in Salt Lake, on what the police and papers called the most dangerous block in the city, with 4 young kids, after getting my arm twisted to come to them and stay at their house instead of heading into California. I was alone still, even though they had promised me acceptance, love, shelter and assistance.

And that isn't even close to the worst of it that night.

As I lay there unable to sleep, someone was murdered right outside my window and made a gurgling sound as they died! The people who did it stood around discussing it for a few minutes afterwards. The words were garbled and muted, almost sounding like animals. All I could tell you is that they were men from the sound of their voices.

The noise of the dying woman and the people the cops chased away later had woken Sha-sha and she asked me what was going on and I quickly whispered, "Shhhhhhh! Don't make a noise, let them think this room is vacant. Shhhhh!"

They responded and chased some people around the building, sounding like a scene out of a law enforcement series.

Another officer called the ambulance and we could hear it like there was no wall there, but it left silently with no flashing lights or sirens, and you know what that means.

When they knocked on my door for my affidavit I told them what I knew, which was mostly just sounds. I wasn't about to open the door with these people right at my window on the sidewalk. And then I looked down at a blood puddle. Gross.

We were there for about a week before I found a place, using my child support income to secure the lease. And a couple of those nights the ghost of the woman who had her throat cut poofed through the closed curtains like powdered sugar on a donut when you forget to hold your breath as you bite it. She just stood there, sort of hunched over, and looked at me woefully.

The first time I put my hand to my mouth and tears welled up in my eyes. And then she vanished as she turned to wander around outside. The few other times this happened I would just look at her and shrug my shoulders.

My kids slept through this every time. I had a hard time sleeping until we left.

If you have to go through Salt Lake City, DO NOT stay at the All Star Motel. You have been warned.

12 Inches Of Ash

After I had lived in the 3rd story 3 bedroom at Logan Place Apartments for a few months, it started to become a little chilly as it was late in the year and winter was coming on.

Turning on the heater didn't just give us the scent of burnt dust, but an odd smell of ashes. Which I couldn't understand. But I *did* understand that my sinuses were getting clogged after running the heater, so I vacuumed out my vents and checked the filter – very dirty so I bought a new one at the hardware store and changed it.

This was something the previous tenant was supposed to do at check out, but no one had even noticed or it would be mostly clean instead of covered with a thick layer of grey dust. Looking at the dirty one a little closer, I realized it looked more like ashes than dust.

Perplexed by this, I went to the huge cold air return vent in the living room. You know the type: those huge vents covering a rectangle hole in the floor or wall or ceiling, probably 3 feet by 3 feet, straight out of 1970. And true to form, this one, sitting near the floor in the corner of the living room had four screws holding it in place.

So I got my screwdriver and opened it up. It was literally 1/3 of the way full of some grey ashes! There were little chunks of bone and tiny balls of lint in there with it. Had a former employee of a cremation facility disposed of all the unclaimed urns in there? Or what? I was dumbfounded.

But after the way I had been treated by 911 dispatch and the officers who showed up at the ER after that rape in 1998, I just didn't think the correct response would occur if I called *this* in.

I might even get blamed for this, even though I had only been living in this apartment a couple of months, and one could tell by the way it was matted down a bit on top that there had been time for settling into that square void.

"This is a job for the Big Green Clean Machine!" I exclaimed, and grabbed my favorite vacuum I've ever owned and powered it up.

"VVVVVVVVVVVVVVvvvvvvvvvvvvvvvvvvvvvvvvvvvvvvvvvvvvvvvvvvvvvvvHHHHHHHHHHHH!"

Just before I plunged the hose in without a nozzle, I heard a voice say, "Don't!"

Too late! Chunks and ash were sucked up into my vacuum, and as some of those little bone fragments ricocheted off the sides of the metal hose extension I knew it was a mistake. So I pulled out.

And then stood there staring at the still massive amount of ash. "So how am I supposed to get this out of here for my sinuses? How about you tell me that, ghost? You think I want to breathe you and whoever else is in here?"

I sighed, put my vacuum back away, and screwed the panel back on the wall.

And any reasonable person would think that was that. But no.

Later when I was dating this rather tall guy from Georgia who had partnered with another guy I attended church with at Saints Connie and Helen Greek Orthodox Church. This business they were partnered in had been only about art and jewelry, but this new guy had convinced my friend to go into debt and buy a huge film developing machine.

We only went on about 3 dates, 2 of which were really just him trying to get into my pants at my apartment, and we never went to the movies or dinner as planned.

And, wouldn't you know it; he also wanted to start a business with me, separate from this friend of mine from church. And just like he'd done with my friend, he wanted me – a single mom of 3 – to fund it all!

On that last date, he really threw on the charm and was genuinely love bombing me. At one point, he had me tipped backwards, off balance for a kiss, and I drifted into la-la land. I didn't realize we weren't kissing for several seconds, until he giggled because he was able to lift me up and down with only his hand under my back, both my feet were off the ground, and I had arched my back into a crescent.

26

The thing that cemented my determination not to go out with him anymore was not this crazy kissing stance he had us in, because that was genuinely funny. It was this overwhelming sense that he was attempting to pilot my mind into this fake investment for his fake business. I was not in the mood to end up in a situation, financial or otherwise.

And also because, soon after that while we were at the table "planning" his fake business and him pushing for me to commit to a certain amount of invested money, there was a loud popping of glass. We both heard it and froze, startled and a little nervous.

We looked at each other. He was genuinely as afraid as I was, maybe more. It almost sounded like a bullet had gone through the window.

I then got angry at whoever it might be, because this is how I process fear. I zoomed over to the balcony and looked down at my car. The windshield was fine, no one had touched it. And so next I looked at my sliding glass door panels. Nothing. I began looking around the room and realized that it had come from the corner of the room where the lamp table was at, *next to* the sliding door.

So I looked down at the items sitting there and saw a pretty shocking sight. The juice glass I had set there had cracked all at once into a perfect peace symbol, and each of those three lines that touch the outside of the circle all followed the glass up to the lip. There is no way that is possible under normal circumstances.

This was not a good sign for me. Because unlike most people, I know that the so-called peace sign used to be an icon signifying Peter's upside down crucifixion, and was the symbol for betrayal.

Not good.

I saw this guy to the door and wished him a nice life.

And I'm very glad I did because he later betrayed his business partner and took off to Georgia with a whole lot of money he'd embezzled.

Whatever/Whoever I had stirred up with my vacuum hose was now loose like a Genie escaped from a lamp. There was the broken juice glass, random noises, some weird visions I had and other odd things that I knew were not done by me or my little kids.

And the most annoying thing they did was to shut off my t.v. any time they didn't like what I was watching. No matter how many times I asked for them to stop, they wouldn't.

The first chance I got, I moved across the street to the townhomes.

The ghost stayed there in the apartment with what was left of it's ashen remains, and everyone else's in there. Maybe.

I had a very odd vision this morning before came in here to finish formatting my manuscript. A black woman about my height and wearing an orange kaftan showed me a living room, gesturing at it like Vanna White on the Price Is Right. And then she flashed her name at me in thick white letters and read it as well, "Joan Kelly" she announced herself.

Now, when I looked up that name there were a good two dozen Joan Kellys of different ethnicity. The ghost I saw looked more like Peggy Kelly, which also popped up on the search. The Logan Place Apartments were mostly inhabited by African American neighbors. And we all know what they've been covering up at some of these funeral and cremation places lately. Shocking and shaking.

Is this the name of the ghost I accidentally sucked up with my Big Green Clean Machine? She didn't say what she wanted or give a message. I guess I wait to find out.

I kind of wonder even still if we were haunted by more than one ghost while we were living there, and if so, how many. It's hard to tell when they are content to just rub elbows with you and not manifest.

13 Repeats

After the adventure with Goh-tu, we got our own apartment and the door number was 113. And it just happened to be the year 2013.

Some people think this is an unlucky number, but I know that it is actually a lucky number, like having a baker's dozen, being old enough to have your bar or bat mitzvah, being old enough to babysit, etc.

This superstition of Friday the 13th being unlucky, stems from a Friday in October that just happened to be the 13th, when the only people that were originally unlucky on that day were the Knights Templar, who got slaughtered on that day in 1013 C.E. At the order of the pope, no less.

Just like a black cat was considered the luckiest cat in ancient European culture because the best soil for growing crops is black. And a black cat running up your walkway and into your house is considered lucky in Scotland, and the omen is that you're going to catch a large windfall of cash. Again, it was the catholic church that contradicted this in the dark ages, claiming a black cat was an evil and unlucky thing. But before them, everyone knew they were lucky. The luckiest of cats to have as a companion or on your farm is a black cat. It's a symbol of fertility and wealth. (In Asia, sailors and fisherman used to say that a calico cat was the luckiest.)

But back on topic, we moved into a basement apartment with 113 on the door. It was a very peaceful apartment until my daughter moved across town (she was in a different apartment in the same complex) and gave me her coffee table. It was a pretty little coffee table, but it came with a spirit who ran around naked and looking very emaciated. And his skin was grey.

Mostly I only saw him out of the corner of my eye and thought I must be tired because he wasn't trying to haunt us actively. But he carried with him a very oppressive and depressed vibe.

I was calmly walking from my bedroom to the kitchen to make food when I saw him clearly one afternoon, spider-crawling and avoiding my gaze as he scurried under the coffee table. I knew immediately that my fireplace was going to come in handy that evening, because that is where that coffee table went. No more grey raisin man.

And then the storm drain in the breezeway flooded our apartment and we were ankle deep in water after a year's lease. But it also spewed back up through the kitchen sink, kind of like something out of a National Lampoons movie. This was a plumbing issue, and not anything to do with my haunted coffee table or the late hero Goh-tu, because the builder had made a mistake back in 1981 when they built the complex and put the wrong sized exit pipe under that stack of apartments. Every year it flooded, approximately June, or so maintenance said. We had moved in at the end of June after they had already cleaned it up and re-carpeted.

Surprise!

So we asked if we could have the apartment directly above us since it was empty and they said yes, no new security deposit required since we were being such good sports about getting flooded.

Now my door read 313. Oh, well. Whatever.

But this place was haunted for sure.

I had seen the police and the caution tape prior to moving into 113 when I visited my daughter. This place had stayed vacant all that year. I don't know why I never made the connection back then when I overheard the housekeeper discussing a haunting with various people at Spirit Pass, a giftshop in our tiny mall which is now out of business.

And later, I had been at the dollar store while the housekeeper was asking someone about how to sage an apartment because she had been experiencing slamming cupboards and noises and yelling from an unseen presence.

I was at the native American themed gift shop again a few days later while she was buying the sage bundles.

I could still smell the sage in the air when we moved in and when I walked into the living room and realized this is what Connie had been talking about when she said the saging hadn't worked and so she drew a cross on the wall.

She had drawn it on the wall of this apartment she had been cleaning! Honestly, I had thought she was talking about her own place. How could she do that when it would affect the new tenant's security deposit. Plus, I could sense that this wasn't helping solve the problem.

I went and found my fingernail polish remover and took it off the wall. Then I got my sage bundle and did a proper saging.

I walked into the front bedroom that ended up being Nikko-kun's room and saw the bleached spot on the floor by the closet and knew immediately that it had been a blood puddle. And I felt the presence of this person and that they were angry and frustrated.

To make doubly sure that the saging was effective, I did every single room, ending in the living room where the front door opened into. And I made a brushing motion to push the negative feelings and this entity out.

And when I was done, I told this sentience that it isn't fair to drag us into it's drama. We were the new tenants and had nothing to do with whatever happened before. "Hang out if you want, but no haunting or harassing."

I shared this with Connie later and her eyes went really wide.

 I mentioned the cross, the sage smell, and the odd spot on the carpet. "Was this the place you were needing saged several months ago?"

She nodded.

"Okay, I'm not trying to start anything, but I included that cross on my check-in list cuz I don't want to be blamed for anything. I've removed it, but it needs painting over in that spot. And we won't be asking for another apartment because I have saged it and whatever it was is either gone now or subdued."

"Oh, good," she sighed. "That one was really hard to clean."

"Well, it's clean now," I answered.

A Visit From The Patriarch

Every other week, during those 365 days I made the mistake of going to Utah to build a bridge between me and my imposter parents, the kids and I attended the Ogden Jewish temple which had formerly been a B'nei Bris building. The other week we would attend Temple Kol Ami.

It had been burnt by an arsonist some decades back, but rebuilt by the congregation attending there in 2002. And it was tiny, but beautifully redone as a little temple. We had a student rabbi who came once a month, and we were working on getting a more suitable temple built.

One week, during the Oneg after the service, everyone was milling about eating and talking and I sat down on the back row in the sanctuary (not the Hebrew name for it) whose doors were still held open, just because my legs were weary. It had been a long week. The kitchenette was tiny and there were a lot of us. I felt it was better to wait for some access to the gnosh by sitting. My kids were able to squeeze in and Mickey came over holding a little plate and leaned on me while he munched away.

Suddenly there was this sound like when a door opens on an air conditioned room, and I started to have a visitation by an old man in Eastern Asian attire – Mongolian clothing I think – wearing an embroidered skull cap with a little pointed tip over the crown of the head and little wings by his cheeks, a heavy robe that looked like a Persian rug, but which was lined with a thick brown fur, like mink, a silk long tunic, and shoes that had the tip that points up. He grabbed a chair about 3 rows away, spun it around and sat down, kicking his robes out in front of him so he wouldn't step on them – that's how I saw the shoes. And also, the other red velveteen chairs were pushed back into a circle with floor space between us. So odd.

I knew instantly somehow that this was Abraham; yes, *the* Abraham. He began gesturing with his hands while he instructed me, but this was telepathic communication, I couldn't hear any sound. I wasn't fully aware of what he was saying, but I knew I was absorbing it.

Next, this other congregant, a guy that looked exactly like Witness's father, but went by a different name now, saw me nodding at emptiness and laughed, I guess he didn't see Father Abraham sitting there. "Are you okay?" he asked.

It was always difficult talking to him anyway when I had known him before in Virginia. Here he was acting like I was just anybody and hadn't given birth to the youngest of his troop there, the same age as Mickey. (You'll learn more about this when you read my autobiography.)

I braced myself and looked up at him standing there and said "I am, but I was just -" I turned and saw that Abraham had vanished and the chairs were all facing the way they were supposed to.

If that wasn't the coolest thing, I don't know what is.

Before I could get up to grab a plate, my daughter brought me some goodies and then went back to her friends.

This rake's wife came to stand next to him where he leaned on the other lintel, glancing at me from time to time. I was angry.

Not only had he come to my house drunk and raped me, saying he missed me. But here was Witness being raised by him and his wife. A wife he wasn't supposed to have. But here she was with 4 older siblings she'd had with this man. I had been used to get a child, and used in the most brutal of ways, and had come home with the one on the news that had been abandoned the month before in front of the hospital. I was angry, but I swallowed it down so deep that one day I might lay an egg like my chickens do.

His wife said, "I thought you said she is the enemy."

He said, "That's because I didn't know this yet. We are fortunate. Not everyone teaches their children the Kashroot."

I have still not figured out why he would say any of this.

I told myself that the most important thing was the Sabbath Peace and the exquisite message and visitation I had just received. And I really needed to gather the kids and head home to try and understand it more.

This kind of ghost most people call an angel or an ancestor.

I was 3 or 4. Nope, 2 or 3. I go back and forth on this by trying to gauge the date by what was going on around me, where we lived and what people were wearing, saying, eating, doing, etc.

Suffice it to say that it could've been both of these years.

Irregardless, I had many encounters, both inside our apartment and outside our apartment in the backyard common area sort of place.

Many times just chatting and pointing to plants. Or eating them in his case. Or playing with my dolls and tea set. Picking up rocks, setting them down.

Mind you, the chatter was mostly noises and baby talk. I was talking with real words, but didn't have it all down yet. Because of this I say that it's more likely I was 2 and/or 3.

When Elaine would come around the corner of the hallway to get me or speak to me, he would grab the edge of the air and pull it over himself like a blanket. This would happen outside as well, but mostly he would just shuffle off into the trees and camouflage when we were outside.

He had dark brown fur and skin like mine when I'm outside a lot. Sort of a dark caramel color. He smelled of cedar sometimes, or dirt other times.

When I would look up at him to say something, or giggle at him, or hand him one of my little teacups, there was a twinkle in those brown eyes.

He was just my hairy friend. I loved him.

And there was a smaller, blue eyed one who spoke English and asked if I wanted to come away with him to his house, or sometimes to his church.

But this other one was shorter, and there was black elastic under the hair of the wrist, kind of like a lunch lady hairnet. You could only see it up close and under the edge of the hair if it shifted just right. And this other one had blue eyes. And like I said before, he would ask me if I wanted to come away to church with him or his house with him and his name was Bob.

Alan caught him one afternoon when he visited in his normal clothing. I don't know if he forgot the suit or just decided that since he wasn't getting noticed by Elaine or Alan so far, he could risk it. And of course, back then I didn't put two and two together. To me back then, the blue eyed furry monster was as different from Bob as the brown eyed furry monster. I mean, what 2 or 3 year old knows the difference between a sasquatch and a giant teddy bear? Or that someone they know is inside that beard and red suit during the holidays? Or that a Yunweh Tsunsdi coaxing them off to it's village is not just another kid?

And I do believe this would be the correct place to insert the encounter at Bob and Shirley's house for the ill-fated playdate with my half siblings, but I will not include it in this publication, and save it for the book about my life.

Moving along the timeline in relation to this cryptid encounter, 1977 seemed to be an eventful year for me. I won a reading contest for the MS read-a-thon for our classroom, and one of the books I read for donations was about an imaginary friend. I laughed at how silly I thought it was, and then Elaine told me about my imaginary friend, Bopawee.

 She said I would be walking back and forth putting things into my little suitcase and my big purse that used to be hers. Then I'd load them up into my toy shopping cart and start going to the door and want to go outside. She would laugh from where she sat on the couch and ask me, "Where are you going?" and I would answer, "Bop a-wee house," or sometimes "Bop a-wee church". And all of us, Mom and my brothers and myself went into fits of laughter.

But now I realize, with that memory stimulated by her retelling, that I was trying to say "Bob away house and Bob away church. Which is a bit alarming. I think my real dad was just going to take me away to live with him. It's his right to raise me, but giving my legal guardians a heart attack and making them think I was kidnapped is completely uncouth.

I really think that Bob was the other hairy friend, that over time I accidentally blended with the memory of the first. And because I was little, the things I noticed, like the elastic at the wrist, and that this other guy's fur was like my troll dolls hair, didn't phase me because I had very little life experience to refer to at that point. I was a pre-schooler, come on. Of course I didn't know. No matter how many times you come back to this rhealm, you start out fresh and blank. Some of us gradually remember things from before, some of us don't. Most of us don't.

But I did compare the different hair, different eyes and different smells of the two. I did notice. In my mind. I didn't feel like it needed discussing. Being small, I had no hang-ups about it and always accepted people with different hair and skin color and clothes and such as they were. It was all just part of the experience for me. And so it just all blended together in my subconscious in it's special little storage place until Elaine drew it forth with her trip down nostalgia lane.

And later, in 1977 I had a very strange feeling when it came to Chewbacca. He looked an awful lot like Bopawee did. And following that, in school we did a unit on Great American Legends, including Paul Bunyan, Johnny Appleseed, etc. And gradually worked our way into the cryptid section of tall tales. Sasquatch, Loch Ness Monster, Leprechauns, etc. The tales of the Sasquatch, or Big Foot, magnetized me. My mind tried to process this and my memories from when I was a tiny little thing in the areas just outside of Seattle and Spokane in Washington. And I think Camas at one time.

Pretty sure I've figured this one out. There was a real one, and then there was my dad in a hair suit.

It's pretty funny if you think about it.

Chanting the Gohonzon

This story isn't a spooky one, but I think that many of you might find it a supernatural gem. I did.

I have a friend named Janet Hirahara who is a practicing Nichiren Buddhist. She included me in some of the ritual chanting and prayer as her friend. But first she had to explain that this wouldn't take away from my worship of the one true God at all, only enhance it.

Nichirens believe that there is one supreme intelligence in the first place. And for them, Nichiren isn't so much a religion as it is a way to enhance your life experience. At least this is the way Janet explained it to me, and I found nothing in my research of Nichiren to contradict this. I even found quotes of other Nichiren that support this outlook.

So one afternoon, after I had been expressing my frustration with life, she offered to sit with me and chant in front of her Gohonzon to see what I might see in my mind and if we could uncover what was causing all of the struggle in my life. She said it might be from a past life, something I needed to account for and set right.

This is when I finally understood how some of what I thought were just recurring memories and dreams were actually my subconscious trying to remind me that I had been here in this rhealm of existence before. The Gohonzon lined them all up together in proper order so I could finally make the connection. Other than realizing that I had been the little girl Sarah in Auschwitz, I had not realized these other oddly misfit memories were from previous lives until that point.

So first we chanted NMRK together for about 5 minutes, and then she chanted the rest and I listened.

While she was chanting the formal Gohonzon, I experienced an interesting thing.

I saw the oldest of my former lives more clearly than before, and the new Groom dragging me uphill, bound around my entire body with a thick rope. My head bobbled as it moved over tufts of grass and I could smell the grass and the dirt. I could feel the sunlight on my face and I saw a whisp of my strawberry blonde hair move across the grass blades as we went.

He was explaining, yet again, how he knew I was innocent, but he couldn't live with the humiliation and the rumors.

I rolled my eyes and silently urged him to just get it over with. I knew exactly which bluff he was dragging me to so he could toss me down to the little brook beneath. Toss me to my death.

I told this to Janet and she was astounded, "You smelled it?" she exclaimed, when I told her I could smell the grass and the dirt.

"Yes," I answered. And then I told her about when I was the 2nd daughter of a Japanese nobleman and I had gotten kicked out of the School of Archery for laughing at my instructor, but I had been laughing at a mistake I had made. And how I couldn't go home again because of the shame, so I was trying to decide where to go as I stood on the dirt road outside.

And how I was a little girl named Sarah in Auschwitz and a few of those details.

And how I was Stephanie Monsanto and was shot by a crazy guy during the premiere of Bambi in a particular theater on the East coast.

The only one I didn't remember at that time was my life in the Sirius star system and the battle I lead to stop those peoples from trying to make a separation by skin color there. And we won....but I wouldn't recall that one until I was gripping the sofa after trying some THC chocolate pieces and discovering how allergic I am to it. My upper lip went blue.

Instinctively I know I've lived more than just these 5 plus the one I'm in now. But I couldn't tell you about them. I think that God feels that for now, these ones are all I need for comparison and analysis.

We're really supposed to focus on the life we're in, and not on the lives we lived before.

The only exception is when it will help us overcome a new hurdle or solve a particularly sticky problem.

I feel privileged to have chanted the Gohonzon with Janet Hirahara.

Cousin Kae In The Storehouse Of Souls

I began to be interested in ESP in the 7th grade, having mostly forgotten about the Fairchild Nursery and the experiments at the University of Utah that I was a part of in the late 60s and early 70s. This new enthusiasm was brought on by the topic of the week in Literature class.

Because I hadn't learned about subtle nuances in body language yet really, I didn't think anything of the teacher and her assistant looking at me an excessive amount during class. I thought that perhaps this was because I got high grades in that class and maybe I was one of their favorites.

 But the assistant to the Literature teacher who started mid-semester also left mid-semester. After she left, I no longer received those smiling glances from the Literature teacher, and the mood of the class changed. Because they were prodding our minds with these topics, I should've been at least a little alarmed. The assistant came out of nowhere and left to nowhere. She looked VERY familiar, but I had known her under a different name I think.

Every time I recall this instance, I wonder if they were expecting me to do something. Something to do with my special abilities. But what could I possibly need any of that for in Literature class, regardless of the topic?

The only thing the two of them accomplished with the ESP unit was making me remember certain things. And a hunger for more information on the topic, so I started checking out books from the public library about ESP, and all related topics.

One book in particular magnetized me: transcendental meditation and astral projection were it's main focus.

Teleportation was cool, but I was only randomly finding myself holding objects I hadn't brought home with me, or finding them set on the floor mysteriously, or on a desk, or whatever.

Somehow I remembered I could see with my fingers, but I didn't remember what that experiment had been about at the Fairchild nursery.

But I decided to play around with it myself and bought M&Ms and held the bag opening away from me so I could test this skill to see if I still had it. 8 out of 10 times I could *feel* what the color was. The mistakes seemed to happen when I would accidentally touch more than one while trying to pluck one out to feel the color and then eat it. Too many colors at once and I wasn't able to nail it down to one. I wonder if I can overcome that.

Astral projection, on the other hand, got my attention because it seemed like an excellent way to be able to chew out adults who liked to regularly humiliate me in public, because if they told anyone they would appear crazy.

Well, I was wrong.

They would tell my parents.

And the first time the woman actually came to the door, I overheard her talking to mom in a panic and got a glimpse or two of her face with blue twilight as her backdrop.

Elaine promised to talk to me, and the woman said, "You can't acknowledge what she did! You have to say something like the holy spirit suggested I check on her well-being."

From the top of the stairwell where I was hiding to eavesdrop, I felt myself make a face. So she could tell my mom about the psychic visit, but I couldn't be told that she had been the recipient? What nonsense. I knew already, I had done it.

I messed around with it a few more times, and then got bored. I wasn't even sure what I wanted to get out of it. There's more on this in my autobiography, so I don't feel I need to put it all in here. But it does lead up to something very much involving spirits. And here it is:

I had an older cousin who was a teenager while I was about 5. Just as he was getting ready to go to college and the rest, he died. Suddenly and unexpectedly, as happens sometimes.

Over that decade I would find myself musing about the situation and wondering if my Cousin Kae was in heaven or somewhere else. Or if heaven is even what everyone thinks it is. And I was thinking about this heavily as I lay on my bed waiting to drift off into sleep.

The transition happened so quickly that at first I thought it was a dream. But looking around I began to feel like I was in a very real place, carpeted in white that glowed with energy and felt so soft on my feet. There was an occasional ripple of mother-of pearl in this energy that pulsed gently through that carpet. Almost every surface was like this in fact. I walked across a foyer into a large room with a curved wall on one side and saw my cousin Kae seated at a long table like the ones for kids in libraries and classrooms. The ones with a white formica top and blond wood on the edges. We sat on these little blond wood chairs, which somehow fit us. The table and chairs were in a little carpeted pit with two steps that wound around the edge of this amoeba shaped area.

In a narrow spot next to windows were short bookshelves with what I thought, at first, were books.

I saw that Kae was reading an old children's book, with illustrations. He wouldn't look at me for more than a few seconds, and wouldn't talk to me. But coming from a family that reads a lot, I thought that it was just reading time and I should go get a book and read it next to him.

So, out of curiosity, I went over to the bookshelves. I picked up one of them – all of which were that same type of white, rippling with energy. Picking one of them up I was slightly astonished that it was more like a glowing white VHS tape case than a book. It wouldn't open. But when you looked at it, knowledge would jump into your mind. If you tried to look directly at it's surface, there were no words or illustrations, only pulsing pastel rainbow swirls behind a white surface.

I tried this with several of them and always got the same effect. One of them I went back to and received a rapid download of knowledge. Surprising.

I picked up another and went down to sit across from Kae again.

I asked him again if he was okay and why he was ignoring me.

He finally looked up from his book and smiling whispered, "I'm okay." And then he quickly whispered an explanation, "I'm not allowed to talk to you in here. It's against the rules."

"Oh," I answered.

I began absorbing information from the box I was looking at, but set it down because I was suddenly aware that two young looking men in white suits were coming towards me.

They addressed me by name and asked why I was there, I wasn't supposed to be there yet.

I asked where there was, and they only answered by telling me I had to go back or I was going to get stuck there and wouldn't be able to leave.

"Okay," I answered, disappointed.

Later I would find scripture that teaches about the righteous souls going to wait in complete silence for Final Judgment in the Storehouse of Souls. And I've come to learn that it is different in appearance for everyone. And yet it is the same place.

We walked towards the lobby I had come from and saw the golden frame around the glass doors. Or, at least it looked like glass. Who knows at this point.

Very suddenly, and with a rush of music in my ears, and the pulsing of pastel rainbow and whiteness, I found myself on my bed looking at the ceiling in the dim light. It was dawn and I could see the first rays of light slowly stretching across my ceiling from my basement window.

I felt like I hadn't taken a breath in a long time. And I felt my lungs slowly fill with air, and my breathing become steady.

I tried to tell this to my parents and they thought it was just a fantastic dream, until I told them that I had read a book about astral projection and had tried it a few times, but around there where we lived. This trip to somewhere else was by accident.

Dad hummed and hawed a little and finally said I should be careful with astral projection because it can be a little dangerous. And I agreed with him.

Now if Kae, and the guardians of the Storehouse of Souls, and myself being a ghost temporarily via astral projection isn't enough spirits for you, take a trip to the liquor store. They have bottles and bottles of spirits. That was sarcasm, in case you're a millennial or a zoomie and you aren't familiar with it.

I don't know why people think that all the ghost stories need to be scary.

Dr. Erin Stone

While my ex-husband Fred was away in Philly doing time in the Brigg (he had failed his pee test for cocaine in his urine – and I still had no idea that he was dealing drugs at that point) and helping decommission the USS Wisconsin, I was woken by a phone call one night that was literally out of this world. Literally.

It came at 2 am or so, which I'm beginning to think is a fated thing for me. Why does it always seem that these things happen at 2 am?

This was in 1991 while I was pregnant with my oldest son.

My daughter was asleep in her new bedroom on her new twin-sized waterbed. I was sleeping soundly on my king-sized waterbed. I hadn't injured my back yet, and to me this was like sleeping on a cloud.

My cute little blue Trimline landline phone rang LOUDLY.

Startled, I sat up immediately in the dark and waited for my eyes to adjust so I could use my night vision as the phone kept ringing in that rattling way it had, louder than a fire alarm it seemed that night.

I stumbled around the bed to the corner where the phone was plugged into the phone jack in the wall, and picked up the receiver only to hear a Chinese guy getting annoyed and shouting in rapid-fire Chinese at some other woman trying to speak to both of us in English – definitely an American accent.

I responded by saying, "Hello? Who is this? I don't speak Chinese. Can I speak to the woman there?"

She says, "Hello? Can you hear me?"

I answer back with "Hi. How can I help you?" There's dead air for a few seconds, not even static. "Hello?"

"Oh! Hello. Good, you speak English."

Sha-sha (my daughter's nickname) wakes up for no logical reason and begins crying.

44

"Is that your baby? I hear a baby."

"Yes," I answer, "She's fine. She's okay."

"Listen, my name is Erin Stone." The static made it hard to understand her, though.

"You're stoned?" I'm still fighting to keep my eyes open.

"No! I'm not stoned. My *name*, my name is Dr. Erin Stone." I could hear a slight whimper in her tone at that point. "I'm cold and scared and I'm far away from home. I just want to get back home safely."

The Chinese guy starts cutting in and out, yelling angrily, but static interfered as well, so his voice seemed muffled.

"Okay," I feel tears welling up because I'm an empath and I pick up easily on other people's feelings. My throat also suddenly starts aching that way it does when the emotions get really intense. "I'll pray for you. Heavenly Father, please help my friend, Erin Stone, to get back home safely and help her stay warm and safe. Amen.....Are you there? Hello?"

There's a short crackle that sounds like she's responding, but I don't know if it's to me or the angry Chinese guy.

And then there's dead silence. Then the call cuts off abruptly and I get a dial tone.

I am suddenly hit with this huge wave of anxiety on behalf of this person and I hang up the phone and set it down on the carpet. I start crying, and I am wide awake now.

Sha-sha is still crying. She must have had a nightmare. I go over to her bedroom and pick her up, comforting her. I carry her to my bed and snuggle her into the blanket.

Then I kneel down and pray some more, leaning on the padded rail on my bed. But then I notice how cold it suddenly is, so I slide into bed next to Sha-sha and pray while lying there. I know it really doesn't matter if we're kneeling while we pray. That's not the kind of thing God cares about when we pray.

I fell asleep mid-prayer.

Over the next few days this woman kept popping into my thoughts over and over, and I kept wondering whether this woman got home okay or if she was stuck in a ditch somewhere. I had no way to know she had been circling the planet and things had gone terribly, terribly wrong.

Until 2014, that is.

On my way to Kentucky to be there for my granddaughter's birth, I spent the night in a hotel. As I settled in for the night I turned on the t.v. and the movie "Gravity" was just starting, starring Sandra Bullock, who I had worked with on a made for t.v. movie years ago when my daughter was just 4 years old. We were both extras.

What a strange circle my life had just made, I realized suddenly, when that scene came up where Dr. Erin Stone is drifting in space in serious trouble and talks to a Chinese guy, hears a baby cry, and then talks to me!!! What?! I unconsciously held my breath for several seconds, taking it all in.

I thought she had made a very miraculous landing because of the way they ended that movie, and that maybe she was a prisoner in a Chinese prison.

I made several phone calls to NASA, the Air Force and any other government bureau that I saw in the telephone book I found in the nightstand which seemed like there might be someone who would know. (On my own cell phone of course, cheaper.) No one knew and acted like I was a crazy nuisance, or passed me to someone else's voicemail. I left messages. No call backs.

I'd really appreciate it if someone would kindly call me from the correct bureau or office and tell me what really happened to Erin Stone.

Especially because this year, I saw an old YouTube video from about 5 years ago, which shows Chinese guys running into a shallow lake full of reeds, just like the one she crashed into in the movie. But then one of them picks up this weird, pinkish, pancake thing with eyeballs in it, and I cringed. "I think that might be Dr. Erin Stone," I mumbled out loud to myself. "Bummer." And then I cried again.

I wonder if she was still alive when she called?

I wonder if I'm correct about that pancake thing with eyes?

I hope I'm wrong and she's still alive somewhere, but now I don't have much hope for it. As quickly as she shot to the surface like a meteor, she was probably dead by the time I was praying for her safe return to her home. And that just sucks.

And I still wish a compassionate person working where she was would get clearance and kindly call me to give me the details. It would help me get some closure on this.

I find it poignant that the night I watched that movie was near my granddaughter's birthday which is at the very end of September, and that my daughter had also been there the night I received the phone call years ago.

Wouldn't it be neat if my granddaughter is the reincarnated Erin Stone? I feel it would be.

And Dr. Erin Stone, wherever you are, spirit or reborn, I hope your next life is beautiful.

Eye Of The Tornado

So, after a series of spooky and stressful events cultivating in an impending divorce, I had succeeded in securing a DITY move from my soon-to-be-ex-husband's shore command. I had the check covering the move. There was just no feasible way to stay there in Virginia with things the way they were between he and I.

Now I needed the moving truck and a car-tow. So I called around pricing all the moving companies in Virginia Beach that were available, after figuring out the correct size.

I'm a loyal fan of U-haul because of my childhood as an Air Force brat, whose father used them the most. But this time Penske had the correct size AND they had an older model in great condition that had a nifty step behind the two seats which was the perfect size for a car seat when placed sideways, and the perfect gap between the two seats for a second car seat. Sha-sha was the right age for a booster and riding up front, so she got to be my little co-pilot in the passenger seat. I had a length of rope and strapped the boys' car seats into their unusual locations nice and tight. They didn't even wiggle.

I got the moving van, the car-tow, the boxes, the tape, and brought them back home, loaded up the truck, strapped the kids in and hit the road. Now, mind you, this was well before GPS and I was using a big fat road atlas. And I was really good at it too.

The trip was like a vacation for me, and the kids didn't know any different. Eating burgers and playing at playgrounds at the rest stops seemed like a huge adventure. Swimming in the hotel pools and eating breakfast in a big room with other travelers was just more fun for them.

And until we got to Nebraska, there were literally no unusual occurrences for even myself to worry about.

But Nebraska was an adventure. Suddenly, around 5:30 pm, the nice sunny afternoon went pitch black with a very heavy rainstorm.

All of the cars and trucks and busses were pulling over to the shoulder and I began to wonder why.

I kept hearing a male voice saying, "You need to pull over." "Pull over." "You really need to pull over."

By the 3rd time repeating it, this voice was so urgent it scared me. So I pulled over. Not that I wasn't going to stop, I was just hoping for an exit and a parking lot, rather than the shoulder of the road.

I could see the tail lights of several cars and pickups parked in front of me further up the shoulder of the highway, as well as a bus and a couple of semi-trucks.

And then I couldn't. I couldn't see anything at all past the hood of the truck! The headlights bounced off the streaks of rain as they slanted further and further to the right. Beyond the nose of the truck was swirling blackness.

Suddenly, the rain streaks were completely sideways and the moving van was rocking like crazy, back and forth.

"God.....I don't know if I like this," I timidly complained. And this is when the whistle of the wind switched to a locomotive engine type of sound.

"Trains? Are we close enough to a train track to hear that?" I asked out loud to nobody but God – cuz the kids were asleep. Which made me laugh.

But then the rocking got fierce enough I felt the whole truck scoot a tiny bit on the gravel on the shoulder – probably about an inch – and I said, "God, I don't know if this is safe. Could you help please? Maybe just some regular rain?"

And the wind and darkness lightened up, so the answer was yes.

The other cars were not there, the pickups weren't there, the bus was missing and the semi-trucks weren't there. It hadn't been more than 10 minutes the whole duration of this strange experience.

I felt silly then, as I was sure they'd gone on down the road while I sat there timidly parked longer than they had found necessary.

It wasn't until I was moved into my new apartment in Midvale and I was chatting with some of my new neighbors about my journey from Virginia that someone educated me as to what sideways rain and pitch black surroundings with the sound of a train meant: I had been in the eye of a tornado.

It doesn't make scientific sense that my moving van sat steady on the shoulder of the road while semi-trucks potentially twice and three times as heavy with their loads of freight blew away, unless you imagine the Creator stepping in and holding us down. That is an experience of biblical proportions.

My entire family forsook me, the Lord still loved me and took care of me. God believes I am worth protecting from dangerous people and the weather alike.

This is why I consider God my best friend.

Fire In The Night

Like any teenager, I slept deeply every night because teenage brains are reconfiguring into their adult formation and therefore need sleep. That's actual Health Science/Biology.

But strangely, whenever something unusual was happening I would wake up and be unable to go back to sleep – even if it was nowhere near me. In such cases, the news would let me know what had woken me up. Most of the time.

Other times I would be trying to solve a subconscious riddle and be caught talking, or sometimes walking, in my sleep.

Like the time mom found me pushing papers around on my 1800s pupil desk and asked me what I was doing. She says I looked right at her with my eyes open and said, "I have a Home-Ec deadline and I have to get this sewn."

She told me about it in the morning and I got an instant flashback of the dream in question, which sent me into a panic only to find that I had two weeks in real time to get this project completed.

Or the time I sleepwalked all the way across the house to the back and almost walked into the air over the staircase, and mom stopped me just in time.

There are numerous funny things I've said to people in my sleep – but thank God I've stopped sleep walking.

Some people say that's a sign of a haunting. I'm not so sure. But this house my brothers and I called the Checker Hop house had a weird vibe to it, and some slightly odd things would occur from time to time.

But I feel that the most alarming night was the one where I woke up to a fire. Not in our house, but directly across the street behind the row of houses there. The grass field was on fire! Every single house on that side of the street was at risk of burning down if my psychic self hadn't shook my teenage brain into full consciousness at 2am.

The first thing that grabbed my attention, outside of myself, was the orange flicker on my eyelids. Had I slept the day away? Was it sunset now? Because the sunset through the windblown branches of our tree out front would kind of make the orange flicker I was experiencing.

I rolled on my side and couldn't drop back into sleep. So I opened them, and the first thing I noticed now was that my white curtains had taken on a strange deep orange hue I had never seen on them before. I lay there trying to process this. And then I smelled smoke. Like a house fire. Was our house on fire!?!? Wouldn't my room be filling with smoke with that gap under the door?! I continued to lay perfectly still, thinking and listening.

If the house was burning, I needed to figure out how to get down to my brothers' bedrooms in the basement. Where exactly was the fire? Wouldn't it have to be in one of their bedrooms beneath me to make my curtains glow? Wouldn't my room be on fire by now?

No, I realized. The faint sound of hungry flames was outside! This made me jump up on my bed to peer through my high-set windows as I pushed my curtains back, and saw HUGE flames, taller than the one story houses across the street.

I started to get my shoes on and some pants, as I was sleeping in one of my t-shirts.

The Wilkes kids lived across the street! Oh my God! And the Olsen's and their son Mike who I had a deep crush on! And the Kunzs! The Ungas in the cul-de-sac which backed up on the field – well, everyone in the cul-de-sac!

Ready to run out and start banging on doors now, I peered southward down my street, a very long one three blocks in length, and saw those giant flames dancing two stories tall behind all those one story homes and billowing smoke stretching upwards into the night sky, blocking out the stars.

"There is no way I'm going to be able to wake everyone up and get them out!" I shouted to God.

I ran out to my find my parents' closed door, banging rapidly and shouting – "Fire! There's a fire! Outside! Help me get people out, quick!!"

Un-dad mumbled "What?"

"Fire, dad! Fire! Get up and help me!"

Their door opened. Dad and Mom both stood there in their beigish yellow p.j.'s with dad weakly asking, "What's this about a fire?"

"DAD! Across the street, behind the houses! We have to call 911! And we have to get people out of their houses!"

"What?!" Mom was finally beginning to wake up.

"It's huge! In the field behind those houses!" I pointed, still trying to step into my pants. My mind was ready to run outside, but I knew my pants weren't yet on.

"How do you know?" Alan was still sleep-stunned.

"Because I saw it out my window!"

Dad finally registered the urgency of the situation, but had to see it for himself. He walked back into his room to look out his high-set windows. "Holy smokes!" he exclaimed.

I dialed 911 and told the operator. And of course, Dad had to take the phone from me and tell her everything a second time. Because that is the way he is.

I finally had pants and shoes on and was starting to go out the door.

"Where are you going?"

"Dad! That fire might get to the houses before the trucks get here, we have to wake people up!"

Both parents looked at each other.

"Dad! Mom! That's why I woke you up! I can't get to everyone by myself!"

"Okay. Good idea. But you stay here in case the boys wake up. We'll go."

"Dad!"

"Just do it."

"Fine."

Both parents ran around in their yellow PJs and knocked on doors. People came out and some of them also ran around knocking on doors. Others ran around to their garden hoses out back and began trying to flood their lawns and wet their wooden privacy fences. I only know that part because my dad told me when it was over and we were talking about it.

I got the congregational directory and started calling anyone with an address on our street.

Several minutes later dad came back and asked me again how I'd known.

"Dad, I told you, I woke up, saw the orange and smelled the smoke. At first I thought *we* were on fire."

"You didn't have anything to do with –"

"Really, dad? Remember me trying to get dressed?"

"Oh, that's right. Sometimes you just know things."

"Yeah. Just like with the hair lip guy who was there to repo the car."

"True."

He got back on the phone. It was the fire marshal. They had located the teen boys that had started it by accident when they got bored at their sleepover. They didn't want to get caught with their firecrackers and jumping beans, so these idiots thought they'd go out in the vacant field.

I can't remember now that I'm 50+ what this kid's name was who was mainly responsible, but I could vouch for him claiming it was an accident, by his reputation.

"Do you know him?" Dad queried, after saying his name to me.

"Yes – well, I don't really know him, but dad, he's a dunce and a klutz. One time he hung his jacket on the fire alarm pull handle. It eventually pulled the handle down, of course. He's the same idiot that knocked me down when he was running for a pass in the hall at school and knocked me out for 3 minutes."

"Oh, that kid."

"Yes. He probably didn't even think about how dry the grass was when he and his friends lit the jumping beans and firecrackers. I'm sure of it. He doesn't think ahead."

The fire marshal wanted to talk to me, so dad handed me the phone. "He's just an idiot, sir," I stated after he told me the whole synopsis. Then he made me tell him everything I told my dad.

"Okay," the man on the other end said, "I don't think we'll press charges, but he's going to have to pay for all the burnt sheds and fences and the edge of a few roofs. Thanks for being alert, young lady."

"You're welcome, good night."

By now the sun was coming up and I started getting ready for school.

No one ever came to interview me from the paper. No one in the neighborhood came to say thanks. I never got the key to the city.

I think, though, that as shy as I was back then, that was fine with me. I saved lives and right before Halloween. Can you imagine all the haunted houses we'd have if I hadn't?

Ghost Dwarf of Tahquitz Canyon

First of all, let it be understood that at the time of the writing and publication of this story, "dwarf" was an acceptable name for people of unusually short stature.

The kids and I moved into a two bedroom after losing the house I was planning to make an offer on which we had been renting. It was the tail end of the Mortgage Crisis of 2007, which they would later claim was the "epicenter" of the Recession.

It's like they never called it a Mortgage Crisis. I hate how they keep doing this. You all know who "they" is.

It was a tight fit, and a lot of our stuff stayed in boxes. There just wasn't room to unpack.

But that was okay, because after 6 months we had given away many items we didn't have room for and moved again to a slightly larger two bedroom in the neighboring town.

And finally, after settling in and getting into our routine with the guys' side of the house and the gals' side of the house, everyone's school and work schedules, it seemed like we had adapted well, and for once there was nothing weird going on.

Oh, I couldn't be more wrong.

It started with randomly appearing brown blood stains in the resin bathtub in the gals' bathroom. They were in the shape of legs, from the glutes down to the ankles. But while the butt area looked to be the average size of an adult, the rest of the legs tapered out rapidly like a dwarf's. Or maybe it was just from a fat kid that had died in the shower? Were they male or female?

This we would find out later.

I would scrub and scrub and they wouldn't go away. Until suddenly they would. A week or two later they were back.

Things began to randomly get flipped off of counters and shelves, desks and tables.

I was almost ready to start filming this for YouTube.

But something kind of cool happened when my cat got pregnant a second time – not a happy event for me – but with this ghost. It became calmer in the apartment. Except the rowdy kittens, of course.

My youngest son was running around with my cell phone one afternoon and trying to record the kittens meowing as they jumped and wrestled and did other kitten things.

Suddenly he comes running into the back of the apartment from the living room and shouts, "Mom! Listen to this!"

What he played back was surprising.

"Let's hit the deck!" the voice said playfully.

"That's not me," Mickey shook his head and looked a little bit afraid.

"You know what? This is perfect," was my response. I took my phone and walked into the living room and played it back for whatever was hiding in the Otherwhere. "So.....here's the deal, sir. I don't mind you hanging out in this apartment now that you've passed on, provided you stop acting like a poltergeist and trying to haunt the place. Capiche? Good." Then I went back to whatever I was doing before.

It seemed that this short guy became the perfect gentleman.

There were no more thrown items, and I think he was helping with the kittens until I could re-home them. They were all mysteriously well behaved.

That's the last I saw of the reappearing bloody leg-prints as well.

I tried to place that voice because it sounded like one of the dwarf actors who were members of "The Uglies" a screen actors guild for short people.

But no matter how many times I played that back, I just couldn't place the voice.

Ghostly Warning

Did I already write about this? I don't think I did. About how I awoke at 2am according to my digital alarm clock, to a male voice telling me to "leave, your father wishes to have you"? Did I tell you about it? Let me check.

Nope.

Okay, here goes:

This ghostly voice told me two more times before I got up and wrapped myself in my bed sheet and dropped silently out of my bedroom window, which was already open for the summer breeze.

I stood there in the moonlight, quietly looking at the back of the house. "Leave for how long? Permanently? I think I need my purse and a few things before I do that." No answer.

So, unsure of exactly what I was supposed to do, I shuffled around the block in the dark, the long route, to Shauna Kelly's house. She was my young women's teacher and she was literally the only person on the block besides God that I felt I could trust.

I was in my nightgown, wrapped in a bed sheet. I was not about to go traipsing all the way across the neighborhood about 4 blocks to Monica Todd's house. No way. Someone was bound to see me in my nightgown and I would never live that down. Maybe even attack me, cuz there was that flasher guy a few months back, right around the corner from where we lived.

I knocked and knocked on her side door, thinking that eventually she would hear me and answer it. Both cars were in the driveway. I think I must've knocked six separate times using that "Shave and a haircut, two bits" tune. No answer. This seemed to be the night for it.

Still very sleepy, I crept into her back yard and snuggled up under the swing set in the soft sand I found there, waiting for my spirit guide to tell me I could go back home. As far as I know, no one saw me walking around the block. All the porch lights were out, and all the curtains were drawn. So no one would've called my dad, I don't think. This was like the time with that black mass.

I lay there, not quite able to go back to sleep the whole time, and watched as my father opened my door, turned on the light, and glared first at my bed, and then at the open window. I stayed frozen, hoping the wind wouldn't even touch my bed sheet or hair. I was far enough back into Shauna's yard that I could see over her low hedges and the short fences dividing all the yards. But that meant he could see me as well, possibly – except it was dark outside and he had the light on. If he saw me, he never gave a sign. He slowly shut my door with a very angry look on his face.

This is what had me believing he was drugging me at night to have sex with me. And sometimes that might still have been true. But I would later find out the needle marks on the vein on my left foot were done by someone else. A pretty infamous someone else. With the complete cooperation and permission of both of my imposter parents.

I wanted to not go home ever again, but I knew that Utah has a policy of forcing runaways back home. (Another reason to hate that state.) And I had tested this trying to run away twice already, a highway patrol officer brought me home the first time, and my parents showed up before I could grab my suitcase out of the back of Uncle Lynn's van and dash through the trees behind his home to a guy named Jeff (according to my cousin Jessie) who lived in a studio on the lot directly through the block from them.

On the way home, I braced myself for a neighbor opening a curtain or a door and seeing me wrapped up in my bed sheet on my way back home. The plan was to sneak back into the back yard and hoist myself back in through my window, but dad was sitting on the porch in his pajamas, glowering at me. Darn it, should've hopped over the short back fence from the irrigation ditch.

As I walked up the sidewalk to the porch, he glared like a demon. I walked as gracefully as possible past him and into the house without saying a word.

I focused on him not really being there in my mind's eye and kept waking.

Do you know that this man never said anything to me about it, nor to my mom, and he never punished me for it. I'm not sure what sort of landmark was made there, but he finally stopped trying to have sex with me.

I am so grateful to God for sending messengers and guides to keep me safe throughout my life.

Grandma Carole

When I was probably somewhere between 1 and ½ to 2 years of age, I had the first visitation I can remember.

Even when I was a baby I had visitations by spirits pretty frequently, but at that time it was still very hard to tell the difference between the living and the souls.

As I got older, I gradually saw these visitors less and less. But I still saw them.

One evening as the sun was still setting, but it was definitely twilight, I saw a very nice woman come into my room. She smiled at me and picked me up. "You take care of my little girl, you hear?" I smiled and nodded.

On the other side of this little room was my Aunt Diane. She was staying with my adoptive parents on a cot. She also saw and heard this woman, and later she told Alan and Elaine about it. But she thought that Grandma Carole was talking to her, telling her to take care of me.

Every so often Alan and Elaine would tell nostalgic stories, because I guess this was a little tradition in their families. Every time we went to the grandparents houses the aunts and uncles would start laughing and talking about childhood adventures, and the grandparents would talk chime in with baby and toddler stories of all the siblings, even though everyone had already heard them all. It seemed like there would be one of these gatherings and storytellings every weekend and holiday when we visited.

We would also occasionally do this at home just the 5 of us, and then 6. So perhaps this is just a form of entertainment from the 50s and 60s that carried on into the 70s. Someone else will have to verify if this is so.

But one of these nostalgia gatherings is when I heard it told and suddenly had a flashback, because honestly, I had forgotten about it temporarily.

It actually triggered my brain to remember things all the way back to the start. And before in some cases.

Even as I typed out this encounter with Grandma Carole, I can see her there, smiling. I can remember us both looking over to Aunt Diane on her cot. And Grandma smiling once more and then she just sort of turned into corn pollen and then wasn't there. And I fell asleep, wondering who she was. Because Grandma Carole had died when Elaine was 12 from diabetes complications, leaving Grandpa Bud a widower with 3 daughters.

This was definitely a ghostly visitation, and a little rugrat saw it with her aunt. And it was a good thing. Not all ghostly visits are bad or spooky.

I hope that if you have had, or do in the future, a visit from a dead relative, that you will consider why they might be there and not be afraid.

Grandma Leona's China Hutch

Similar to the piano, there's another piece of furniture that a dead relative made sure I received.

I have a very fuzzy memory of looking at this item in it's original state at Grandpa Joe's house. It's an antique, dark wood, I think cherry, and it has been through a lot, but it's still very pretty and in good shape.

Let me tell you all the anecdotes.

First of all, I was so little when my adoptive grandma, Leona, handed me off to my adoptive parents while my mom was at school, that most of my baby and toddler days with her faded off into my memory storage in my mind.

But while I was still married to Carl, I started remembering her.

Specifically, I remembered my mother, still only 14 with her hair bleached blonde, holding me while we stood in front of this pretty little cherry wood piece and murmuring in my ear, "We'll get this hutch if we play our cards right." And also noticing that we were reflected in the little glass panes of the doors on top.

But remembering that made me confused, because I had seen that very hutch at Uncle Lynn's and Aunt Carla's house when we went to stay with them the winter after un-dad's business failed.

I thought it was so funny when my cousin David had decided one of the little squares of glass was the perfect place to stick a 1776-1976 sticker. The bicentennial was a cool thing. But Aunt Carla went berzerk almost, screeching at him and then going to find a steak knife to try and scrape it off the glass.

Un-dad looked at her and asked her why the two doors didn't match, one with 6 panes and the other with a long solid rectangle.

She told him how she'd accidentally tripped while holding her mop and the handle had smacked through that door like it was only a thin sheet of ice over a puddle. I tried not to laugh. Because Aunt Carla was always doing things like that. When she said she tripped on the mop because she stepped on the yarn end, I actually saw a little vignette play out in my mind. It's very hard not to laugh out loud when you see an image like that.

She said that when she had a guy come to look at it, he had told her he could replicate the 6 paned door, but he'd have to match the wood and get all the little squares cut by another guy and it was almost double the amount if he just took some glass he already had and fit it in the door frame in one big piece, so she let him.

And then, she painted it this god-awful lime green chalk paint over top. Supposedly this looked better. I didn't think so. But I didn't say anything. I had become accustomed to the prevalence of army and lime green coupled with goldenrod and orange. Mostly goldenrod. This might be why I have an aversion to these two shades.

At any rate, I barely noticed when un-dad mentioned that he thought I was supposed to get the hutch. I was about 13 at the time, and what did I need a china hutch for?

But Grandpa Joe and Leona, even though she had thrown me to the wolves, had wanted me to have it because this hutch circled back to me later. Much later.

And I have to take a side track for a minute to tell you about this friend of real-Alan's who loved to steal cutlery from your table as a prank, and then the next time he'd come for dinner he'd say, "Missing a piece?" and there would be all kinds of corollary about the playful theft. And then he'd steal a different piece to bring back the next dinner. He did this to everybody.

So years and years later, after I had moved to this little town, one of my facebook friends asked if any of us could come help her move stuff out of her storage to her little house in town. A couple of us volunteered and met her there.

The other person came with a pick-up truck and right away tried to start something with me by saying that I needed to get caught doing something so I could be punished. Which is when I realized why she looked familiar. She was the driver of one of about 6 vehicles that would gang stalk me all over the place. I had begun recording tags, date and time on them all.

So I looked at her, turned and grabbed my notebook out of my dashboard, and flipped to the most recent page with her tags on it. "Yup!" I exclaimed. "Did you know that it is a felony to gang stalk people?" And then I showed her the entry with her tags.

She froze, she sent a text, received one and then said, "I gotta'' go", and peeled off.

So Michelle, the lady emptying out her storage said, "You can have this once we're done," as she laid her hand on the back of this cherry wood hutch.

"Really?"

"Yes. You didn't take off on me."

"Okay."

The time came to ante up, and I don't remember which of my sons was helping that day, but we tilted it back into the van and slid it up in there. And heard the clatter of silver utensils as we did so.

Michelle closed her eyes and shook her head.

"I'm sorry, did you want those?"

"No!"

"Oh, okay"

The two of us, my son and I, climbed into the van and took the hutch home.

As we slide it into position against the wall, I notice the color, then have that flashback, then notice the mismatched glass doors, then the Bicentennial sticker.

Weird.

Then I open the drawer and notice all kinds of mismatched eating and serving utensils. Most of them look like your typical aluminum cutlery. A few are silver. And then there's the stainless steel butterknife we never could find out of a set mom and dad had from their wedding until today. The missing butterknife, complete with rosebud pattern on the end and the filigree on the sides.

So the question remains: was it Grandpa Joe, Grandma Leona, real-Alan, or who? Which one of them orchestrated me getting my china hutch I was supposed to inherit?

It's like an inside joke from the otherwhere.

Green Monsters

There was a period in my life when I was terrified of these green monsters I could see sometimes in the dark that could read your mind. They looked kind of like Jim Carey's version of the Grinch.

But as a kid, I just knew that if you covered all of your skin with your blanket or a bed sheet they weren't allowed to. Or maybe they couldn't? Something about their ability depended on seeing part of you. I was about 6 or 7. And I thought it was maybe my imagination until I overheard a few conversations of friends and in passing. Then I began to wonder.

I've tried to research it at the library and online, and really haven't found anything. I've also shared it in various settings to see if anyone else has experienced anything like it, nothing. No one wants to tell me if they have experienced this.

EXCEPT when talking to people who have tried shrooms and mescaline. For some reason they all see the same weird creatures. Little people that some of them call elves. The Jesters. And green monsters. Tall, sometimes hairy. And green. Like a lime.

Being a tetrachrome like I am, I see colors others don't. I see shades that others don't and will find two fabrics in a color or two sheets of paper in a color that everyone else will say match, while I feel that they don't. One will often look slightly lighter than the other, or a little bit more of a color than the other.

Sagebrush when it turns beige will also have a sort of purple glow around it for me. And there are other things that I've experienced this from.

Like a large piece of Citrine I have which glows a nice salmon orange for me, like red salmon. But when I take a picture to share with others, it only glows that standard powdery blue like Citrine is supposed to on low frequency blacklight.

So I have been wondering lately if this is why I can see spirits and cryptids when others don't see anything at all, without the aid of drugs. And it would be interesting to find other tetrachromes and discuss whether they have psychic abilities as well.

It's a theory of mine now.

Haunted Trucking School

Oh, my gosh, I just thought of another one.

So, I got fed up with office work, heavy workload like a boss, pay like a janitor.

I tried a few other things, not satisfied.

Got an email complimenting me on my excellent driving record. So, flattered cuz the insurance didn't seem to care, I called this trucking school. It was C. R. England in Utah.

Now, I should tell you I have a great hatred of Utah for a number of personal reasons. Creepy, scary, racist, murdering weirdos, type of reasons. I don't go to Utah if I don't have to.

Anyway, when the recruiter tells me she's sending me to the Utah school instead of the Michigan School, I literally heard that crazy music they play in psycho: "NYAH-NYAH-NYAH-NYAH!" Nearly passed out on the phone. But I held it together. Needed a break. Changing career paths is tough.

So I go out there, and this place is where they had a juvenile detention center for a while, then they built a different one and sold to C. R. England.

One day I go into the women's showers to get clean, and on my way to the shower section, I have to pass the toilets, and I see this little kid standing in a toilet stall.

I'm like, "What?"

I go to ask him if he's lost and what he's doing here (this place is all adults), and he looks up at me and then he's suddenly not there. He wasn't a detention youth, I'm telling you, a little boy, like a one year old. And that is probably the weirdest thing I experienced there.

But people who went there will tell you some of these things: The showers would turn on in this place by themselves, (old fashioned knobs), the faucets turn on full blast – and these are the ones you have to turn on with your hands not the newer automatic ones, the auto towel dispensers roll out towels when no one is near them.

The Time I Was Mistaken As A Ghost

It's a bit of a tragedy (which only I seem to care about) that when I was 15 years old I was sold by my imposter parents to a vitsa made up of South American Gypsies, Travelers from Europe, and some Eastern European Romany, and then somehow ended up being in the clutches of Jeffery Epstein. However, with the exception of a few of these gypsies, they were mostly U.S. Citizens.

Let me tell you:

I had met a cluster of teen boys from this vitsa, being tailed by their younger siblings as happens in every ethnic group, at the public swimming pool in Orem. (I only recently found out a certain woman I call Clownfish coordinated both they and I being at that pool together.)

There was some flirting, but I was still shy back then. They had their fat little cousin come ask if I liked one in particular and I said yes, but I didn't know him well and that I am shy at first. So he told them.

This youth was only a little bit older than me, but when his fat little cousin told him what I said, he blurted, "Shy means she's not interested."

And then the fat little cousin said, "I'm gonna marry her." And then he floated over to me on his donut floaty and told me. And I told him that he was too young for me.

A few minutes later the teenager in question came up behind me on the pool deck where he saw me leaning against the side of the pool and asked me himself if I was interested.

Not knowing that this is the first step to having the parents meet and discuss betrothal and marriage in a vitsa, (traditionally) I innocently said that I was interested.

He asked why I wouldn't look at him and I looked up at his chocolate brown eyes and said, "I am. But I'm shy at first when I meet people. I need to get to know you." And then I shyly looked back at the water.

He asked why. So I answered, "I don't know but I get scared, well, nervous, and I get butterflies in my stomach." I couldn't look at him a second time.

He and his friends laughed and commented how cute that was. I told them to stop laughing because I couldn't help it. And then he said, "Yeah, she's the one." And then they all ran off together somewhere.

I looked at the tiny waves in the pool in front of me and asked no one, "I'm the one for what? What did I do?" And this made me nervous that I was getting blamed for something and so I decided it was time to go get dressed and go home.

I gradually forgot about them all and went on with my 15 year old life.

My imposter father made inappropriate comments to me several days later and I got very sarcastic towards him. He said I was disrespectful and he was going to sell me to the gypsies. This man is known for making bigoted jokes and comments, and exaggerating things for what he thinks is humor. I thought he was just being a jerk again and I sassed him. Nobody sold their kids to gypsies, he had told me that. It was just an ethnic slur.

Well, he was actually serious. It had all been arranged behind my back by the Grandfather (the Patriarch of the vitsa) and my imposter father.

I've done my research, and it's customary to have the parents of the bride and groom meet and a dowry agreed upon. But this dowry is paid to the parents of the bride. Which makes this like a sales transaction. The bride then goes and lives at the home of the groom and spends time with the groom's mother, and they make all the wedding plans, and the groom's mother picks the dress the bride will wear and everything. But the bride is there while this happens. Normally.

But not for me.

As I relayed to anyone listening in one of my YouTube videos, it all started with a glass of milk given to me by my imposter mother. This glass of milk was laced with Spanish Fly. It's also known by another name, but we'll leave it at that, because that other name gets used way too much lately.

It was brought to me while I was doing my homework, which surprised me, because that woman never did that kind of thing. In fact, no one did. Not for me. I accepted it in surprise and began drinking it. I was so psyched to be in high school. Four more years of this and I could join the Air Force, go to college, and start my life. My goal was to keep my grades up and sail on that. The school year had just started and I was off to a good start already. It was September 1982.

My imposter mother started to leave, seemingly depressed and worried. But she was always depressed and worried about something, so I tried to ignore it and concentrate on the assignment in front of me. But instead of leaving, she stopped and turned to me, leaning on my door frame a little.

As I looked up at her she asked me, "Remember when I told you that if you're having a bad dream you can change the channel?"

I answered, "Yes. I like that one. It actually works."

"Well," she continued, "Sometimes the dream won't change no matter how hard you try. And that's when you should just step back and let the dream happen. Just tell yourself it's just a dream and it will be over soon."

In some of the situations I was put into later, heavily drugged with sleepwalk drugs, this may have saved my life. My brain took her advice to heart and I just tried to find a way around the danger, or back to my home.

I looked at her and scrunched my eyebrows together, "Okay. Has that happened to you?"

"Maybe," she murmured. "Just remember that. No matter how scary it gets, it's just a dream. Ride it out until it's over."

"Okay, thanks mom." Then I went back to my homework. Until I felt very, very sleepy and wondered if I had stayed up too many nights in a row from Friday through Sunday. I saw that she had left, got up and shut my door, and then cleared my bed which I had been using as a desk. "Oh, that's nice, " I mumbled as I stretched out on my stomach and dropped into Wonderland.

I kept having the craziest "dreams" that night. (I would find out much later that it was more than one night.)

First I "dreamed" that all these women and teen girls were fussing over me and trying to get me to wake up. They were doing my hair and makeup and trying to get me into a dress. Someone told someone else to go get me some coffee. "I don't drink coffee," I told them. "She doesn't drink coffee. What should we give her, she has to wake up for the ceremony." "Please, look at her. She's so drunk she won't even taste it. Just give it to her and tell her it's something else." "Okay." They made me drink something, probably coffee. And they were right, not only could I not taste it, but I couldn't feel the wetness of the liquid. I know I swallowed in this "dream", but I didn't feel the liquid move down my throat. I did feel a warmth in my belly, so something was down there getting digested. I'm a very lucid dreamer much of the time, so that leant to my assumption that all of this was a "dream". A very weird, annoying, clamoring "dream" full of women doing what women do and driving me nuts.

Oh, don't get me wrong, I love girly stuff. I like makeup and jewelry and perfume and looking pretty, but not to the point of having an entire army of women dolling me up. I'm a tomboy. I am normally found out in the woods or hiking a trail or digging in the mud. I only get dressed up for special things or worship. Or the office when the job requires it.

Next thing I know, there are these two teen girls helping me get down the aisle in a chapel, and I kept tripping. I was tripping on the hem of the dress, my own feet, and possibly nothing at all. I was still in a "dream" state and everything was cloudy around my vision, like when there's too much chlorine in the swimming pool and you see those wisps of white floating around in the water, and then your eyes get red from the chemicals.

I kept falling into the ends of the pews and my face would nearly collide with someone's head sitting in the pews. And I would ask them, "Are we at a wedding? Who's wedding is this?" And then I would hear a bunch of people laughing.

I could see white chiffon or something puffed up from my shoulders, but it didn't make sense that it was my wedding. I would've known if I was getting married, wouldn't I? Doesn't a bride need a groom? I didn't even have a boyfriend yet.

Finally we reached the end of the aisle and I was propped up in front of the pulpit as the priest came and stood in front of me.

There was a commotion at the back of the chapel, but I was too busy trying not to fall on the ring boy, and as I slid down his little chest, I saw a light blue and navy plaid bow tie, and that he was wearing a baby blue vest right before I lost consciousness again and face-planted into the beige carpet.

The next "dream" found me propped up on a folding chair and I kept asking everyone who would listen if they would help me find a couch or a bed so I could lie down. No one would do it, so I pulled out the chair next to mine and put my feet on that and then slouched into the one I was sitting on until I could feel the rim of the chair back on my neck.

This blond guy who was dressed very nice and looked to be about my age came and tried to talk to me. He asked if I wanted to dance and I begged him to help me find somewhere to lie down. He tisked and walked off. I saw him talking to a couple of girls and found myself standing next to the three of them where I heard him say, "Look at her, why should I be with someone so disrespectful?" And I looked over at myself slouched in the two chairs. Had I left my body for a minute?

I found out later they were trying to have him stand in as my groom because the original groom had run off from the church with his three friends when he saw a blonde at the pulpit. This was the guy I had met at the pool. (I am not naturally blonde. When I returned home later I wondered why my hair was so light and was told it was from girls' camp. That the sun had done it.)

In the next "dream" I was flopped onto a bed and various wedding guests, men and youth of all ages, kept coming into the room and using my body. The very first of which was Jeffrey Epstein. (Why was he even there?) And this creep also tried to teach the ring boy how to stimulate me after he wandered into the room where Epstein had my skirt pulled up in the front. Epstein, had me propped up on his chest, sitting between his legs, and had also unzipped the back of my gown so that my nipples were exposed and I was uncomfortable and cold, and I kept complaining about it. Which he ignored.

The ring boy found it boring and left. And then Epstein lifted me up so he could push the back of my gown up over my hips and then sat me down on his member. I lost consciousness again while he was gently lifting me up and down like a ragdoll.

At some point I was moved across the hallway to a different room, because I noticed the door was on the other wall. I tried to sit up several times, and when I finally did I noticed there was a red lipstick on the nightstand next to the bed. I slipped my arms back into my sleeves and stood up. I made a tally mark on the wallpaper – huge magnolia blooms on a dark green background, and then started to head for the door. I needed to get out of here. I don't know why the tally marks made sense at the time.

But before I rounded the foot of the bed, I thought I'd better hide the lipstick in the drawer in case they brought me back. Don't ask how I keep knowing things ahead of time, I'm not really sure. Even under the influence of this drug, this still works in my mind, the knowing of things in a precognitive way.

Being able to choose things? Having the seriousness of something register with me, random. Sometimes I can grasp it, sometimes I'm on a surf of whatever they gave me, bobbing along on a sea of dreams.

I stumbled down the hallway, and a woman with short blonde hair stopped me and asked where I was going.

"Please," I requested. "I have to get home. I have school in the morning, and this isn't really a good environment for me. I'm only 15."

"I can't," she answered.

"Please," I begged her.

She told me I would have to ask the Grandfather, who was sitting in that large room at the end of the hall with a huge window behind him. I asked him, and he pretended to not know English and the blonde girl translated for him.

"He says to take you back to your room," she told me, smiling kindly. And then she took me by the elbow and started me back down the hallway. I had to make it the rest of the way by myself in that condition.

I actually found the door I'd left open and fell over on the bed. Men would come in and use me and leave. They were sweaty, drunk, grotesque and had stubble on their faces. Gradually, I would sit up on the edge of the bed, make another tally mark and then stumble down the hall to the

Grandfather. I made 7 or 8 of these lipstick tally marks before accomplishing my goal to leave.

At some point between all these petitions to be returned to my home, the blond groom – the stand in – sauntered in and stood examining me. He looked me over, pacing a slight distance at the foot of the bed, and then stopped again.

I watched through my eyelids that I could only open a little. I was confused, what was going on here? He picked up my left foot, which had lost it's shoe, and looked at the top of it. He saw the several needle bruises which I would not see until much later after I was conscious.

The light dawned in his mind, and I could see this on his face. "You've been drugged!" He exclaimed.

"Ya' think!!" I almost shouted, by now realizing this must be the problem. "Help me get out of here."

"I can't," he smiled. Then he dropped my foot. Smiled at me from the doorway, and then left.

I immediately forgot that I was not in a dream. It looked and felt like a dream, my brain insisted it was a dream.

The final time I made it down the hall, I told the Grandfather that I needed to get back to protect my brothers because my father would do things to them sexually if I wasn't there as a shield. He had already done this before. And otherwise he normally did this only to me.

I watched this man's face wash over with disgust. Then he said in English, "Help her get her things and go home."

Now I was tarnished goods? After all the guests had been toying with me like a party favor? And what about the groom? What about his orgy in that other room? The second groom, the stand-in guy.

But that is not what I was thinking at that time. I had a pretty one track mind then. I needed to get home.

Now this young woman had become noticeably concerned. She helped me back to the hallway, told me to go back to my room and wait. Then she went looking for her coat.

I tried to go back to my room, but I think someone had shut the door. I didn't see the light shining out onto the hallway. So I steered my tottering self into a room on my left where the door was open, and it was full of laughing young people. Maybe they would help me find my way.

And then I noticed that they were carousing in various states of undress. I'll let you use your imagination as to what else they were doing.

The blond guy who had been selected as a stand in for the runaway groom looked over and saw me there and yelled, "Slut! I'll kill you if you don't get out of here!"

Oh, suddenly the "dream" was becoming dangerous. I was *not* getting killed in my dream. I tried to spin around but only stumbled backwards on the hem of my dress and fell onto my rear end, arms propping me up.

He untangled himself from the myriad of girls clinging to him and started to chase me out into the hall as I picked myself up.

What was happening? I tried to run and fell twice. The stand-in groom laughed and went back into the room he was in before.

I kept running until I was somewhere a little past my door, and it was closed. Or rather ajar. A couple was using my bed, I noticed, as I peeked in through the crevice between my door and the door jam. The tally marks were there on the wall, but I decided I didn't need them anymore.

(These same tally marks were seen again by me as I watched an urban explore of this place clear back in 2019 or 2020 I think. Maybe it was Josh Explores? I can't find it again. If this guy could help me, I'd like to cut that square out of the wall and frame it as a souvenir. Those tally marks are mine, and the building is abandoned anyway.)

I stumbled the rest of the way down the hall until I found a winding stair case and clung to the railing as I sort of walked very sloppily down them, almost falling several times. I'm so lucky I didn't die that night.

I must have blacked out again, because the next thing I "dreamed" was stumbling down a dark road next to a lake and wondering what lake it was.

And then I was walking into the lake at the edge of a small inlet, until the lake was up to my waist. Why couldn't I feel the wetness? I could see the water. All black in the moonlight. What does this dream mean, I thought. And I fell asleep.

I awoke feeling cold again, why did this come and go, feeling cold? And realized that I was not lying on a pillow, but was resting my cheek on the water. Ugh. Why was I "dreaming" I was walking in a lake? What did this "dream" mean? Gradually as I walked (mostly swam) across this little inlet, maybe the width of your average driveway, the bottom got higher and the water got lower. And then I was on the shore. But I'd torn my dress and gotten it dirty and that was annoying.

"I just need to go back to my home in this dream and everything will be okay. It'll all go back to normal. I should find where my home is in here," I told myself out loud. (In here meant inside the "dream".)

I kept stumbling down the road, the bushes and trees to my right. And then I saw a car on the opposite side of the road. They had stopped and were looking at me and pointing.

"Oh, good. Could you give me a ride? I need to go home." I said, weakly. I don't think they even heard me. I was even with the driver's side door, but still near the edge of the road on my side, so I reached out to wave and tried to ask again for a ride. But neither of them was looking at me anymore. They were looking at each other and talking.

I dropped my hand to my side and waited so I could get their attention. No good. I could feel myself needing to lie down again. I looked over to my right and there was this nice fat shrubbery with a smooth area of dirt under it's branches. I crawled in and curled up under it and fell asleep again.

The next thing I "dreamed" was of Jeffrey Epstein nudging my shoulder, opening my eyes and seeing him smiling at me. "There you are," he grinned, and then extended his hand. I took it, started to stand up, and then fell asleep again. And at that point in time, I never knew his name.

There's 87 more days to this side of the story, but you'll have to read my memoirs.

Let me just wrap this story up with what I found out about this guy whose face I never forgot, it was Kevin Sorbo. When he played Hercules, I couldn't figure out why he looked so familiar to me.

Until I was watching Celebrity Ghost Stories years later, and he related the tale of how he'd been on a date when he saw a ghost bride. I've been wanting to tell him ever since I saw that episode in the series, "Hey, Kevin, it wasn't a ghost bride. It was a living bride who was soaking wet and needed a ride. It was me. "

But when will I ever get a chance to tell him? I don't travel in his circles and have no plans to go back into the land of the crazies which is California. I know his talent agency is in New York, but I really don't feel like going there either.

Maybe I'll just send him a copy of this book.

Kitchen Spirits and Tea

There was another night I got woken during the wee hours. As I got older, I would come to be more and more familiar with this phenomenon.

But this was one of the first times and I was confused. Why was I suddenly awake?

I went up to the kitchen almost immediately, and suddenly felt the urge to crouch down behind the cabinets which lined either side of the galley kitchen in the white brick house. It felt like someone or something – and more than one of whichever – was out in the backyard. And it was trying to come in the back door but was restricted somehow. In that moment, I knew it was spirit, and not nice, either.

So I did something I vaguely remember doing in the Fairchild Nursery, which was to send out a wave of energy that would make it uncomfortable. It worked a little the first time, but I had to increase the "pump" of energy 3 more times before it surrendered and left. If it had spoken, it's response would've been something like "Fine! I'm going." This came in the form of a wave of energy interpreted as acknowledgement and compliance.

I had clenched my teeth and included physical contraction of several muscles, and now I had a headache from it. So I got myself a glass of hot tea with milk and some aspirin. As I was finishing my milk, dad came in and asked why I was up.

I told him everything, doing my best to describe the indescribable.

He was dumbfounded, but his reply was that there probably was something bad outside.

I got a chill down my spine when he said that. I think he knew exactly what that something was.

See, he knew what I had gradually forgotten about myself during my childhood. He was one of the men at the University of Utah. He was the one that had murdered Alan because he wouldn't put me back in that program after they accidentally electrocuted me during an experiment. And then took over his life.

As most of us do, I had tucked memories of my childhood very safely away in my mind. The thing that makes me different than most is the frequency with which I am able to access these memories and mull them over until I find the details I need. All I need is the right scent or words or song or t.v. program and I have a flashback. And if none of that happens and I want to remember something, I can usually sit still and think about it for awhile and it will resurface. But standing there in the kitchen at about 2am, putting my glass in the sink, the memories lay dormant.

Dad looked uneasy as he queried, "What are you going to do now?"

"Go back to bed, job's done," I mumbled.

And then I almost silently padded down the carpeted hall and the stairs and glided across my bedroom to slide into my bed onto my stomach and find dreamland.

Lightning Fingers

There had been a series of lightning strikes that season of various individuals, all of whom had survived, including a mother while she was heading to her car in a parking lot, and a teen boy who had been wearing his earbuds when he was struck – with all that was left of them being two copper pills nestled in his ear canals.

That kind of story just stays with you. They're just so alarming.

Well, evidently, I was foolishly about to make myself the next fried fool, walking from my car with my cell phone in my purse, and on. Clouds were in the sky, but it wasn't raining yet.

I was headed into Murphy High School to register my daughter for the coming school year, when I saw a movement in the sky headed my way and looked up to my right, just in time to see a thick tube (It was tubular, what?) of electricity smack into something silvery, shimmery and transparent, right next to the roof over the second story of the gymnasium.

Flabbergasted, I watched that thing split against this energy umbrella (for lack of a better word) and branch into 5 fingers of lighting! One of these fingers hit the traffic light at the end of the street and shut it down, another smacked a thick branch off of an old tree, and the other three, I have no earthly idea what they struck.

I ran the rest of the distance into the main building and texted my kids not to worry if I didn't answer for awhile, I was shutting off my cell phone for my safety.

I registered my daughter for her classes.

Then I just stood there in the office watching out the window until I had the courage to make my way back to my car.

Was this a wake-up call for something I'd forgotten? Or was it simply God looking out for me?

Either way, I was protected from a force of nature by the one who made it all in the first place, and this is yet another reason why I claim him as my best friend.

Ma Belle, Yisraelle

Because I thought I had a job lined up, I moved us from California to Alabama. That old friend who knew a guy thing didn't pan out, though.

A friend I had while married to Fred, and who had also been a navy wife, had told me there was a job for a paralegal at a firm in Mobile. This was a vaguery that I somehow believed was a connection, called them, sent a resume, did a phone interview and was told that I could start as a receptionist, and in about six months his paralegal would retire and I could move into her slot.

There were no apartments available, and the one I thought I had got us on the waiting list told me, "We don't do waiting lists."

This was post Katrina mess, not during. Alabama seemed like she was savoring it. Letting it slowly melt in her mouth like she liked it. Well, I did not.

I finally found a house for rent one block from Water Street. I thought because we were in the south that this 2 story shotgun structure was all for us for the rent we were paying. It was not.

Only the top half or the bottom half.

Well, the top half had considerably more room and a balcony – which turned out to be unsafe- but was at the top of a long flight of suicide stairs. We had to drag our washer upstairs on a blanket, and also our fridge.

But downstairs only had one bedroom. And humongous windows that everyone could look into straight to the other side, and this house was right on the corner. With the crazy mess we had dealt with in California, the crow's nest sounded so much better to me.

Boy, was I right. We had a 12 month respite from being stalked, no one who came looking for us realized we were upstairs. The bottom apartment was unoccupied for the first 4 months, we had neighbors for 2 months, and then the final 6 months it was empty again.

Of course, guys I dated didn't realize I was upstairs, postal deliveries were confused by the empty downstairs and left things in the little lobby. And people we worshipped with who came to visit got angry and thought we told them a false address.

Only one time in that whole year did anyone notice us upstairs, and that was a guy in a little white ½ size pickup with a girl by his side.

I was standing in our tiny kitchen drinking my coffee one morning and caught him looking up into that tiny window at just the right moment. He was a little rude about it to, did the pump fist at me.

It was so peaceful up there, though.

Even our resident ghost was peaceful. I never did find out his name for certain. He was a black guy who would drift up to the bedroom I shared with my daughter from downstairs and outside by some bushes.

The guys shared the other one at the front.

He always said the same thing to me in French, "Ma belle, Yisraelle." And he would repeat it 3 or 4 times every time. Because of where I saw him drifting up from I began to suspect some foul play. Because of the clothes he was wearing, I guessed it might have been early 1900s.

See, there was this row of little shrubs that were lined up at the back of the house with an awkwardly wide gap between the row and the back of the house. And it didn't travel from corner to corner like one would expect, but was just barely long enough to be the length of a man between 5'8" and 6' tall.

This is what drove me to find the archives for the city.

And I never did find any firm facts on him.

But I did discover that there were 20 families of Jews who disappeared in the 1800s, and that the Masonic Temple on Water Street was first a Jewish Synagogue. And that Jewish families arriving in Mobile after the Civil War ended, to try and locate their friends and family found this changed and openly accused certain people they found using their friends' and families' names of not being the people whose names they were using. In fact, I found a good half a dozen of these entries.

But on the lighter side, I found out that the armory which manufactured bullets used to sit right there on that lot, but facing the other direction. And that after that it had been a dressmakers facing the way it was now.

My gentleman ghost remained anonymous and a gentleman. Always calling me his pretty Israelle. That's what "Ma belle, Israelle" means.

Maybe He Just Needs Love – NOPE!!

While we were living in Magna, I developed another reason to hate the place.

See, in Magna, there were a few odd things I experienced, but mostly put to the back of my mind until I got older, which still perplex me today. The one regarding our pets not being there, and then suddenly they were again was the most odd to me.

The yellow parakeet I had named Sunny came with us, but she was never in my bedroom in Magna, or the living room, or anywhere in the house! I remember carrying her into the Magna house in her cage, and I remember un-mom saying she should stay in her room for awhile – but I don't remember hearing her chirping or anything after that. Or changing the paper in her cage. Or letting her fly around my bedroom. I've scanned my brain on this. She wasn't there. But she was there, club foot and all, in my bedroom at the Checker Hop house and at the white brick with blue trim in Orem. And then she died and I buried her there. It's an anomaly.

The black terrier that my little brother had named Heather was with us in our back yard when we had our fire pit in Magna, and then was just never there as I came home from school, or while we were moving. She just wasn't present. Until we were in Orem and she was chasing my brothers and their friends around in their cub scout uniforms because she hated any kind of uniform for some reason. Any kind of uniform. UPS, Mailman, Cop, Cub Scout, teenagers walking past our house dressed for McDonald's or Burger King. If you wanted to be safe from Heather, you had to wear your street clothes.

The encounter with the devil, however, was the scariest thing, by far.

And good old Warner Brothers kind of set me up with that cartoon episode about Wiley Coyote and the Sheep Dog not really being enemies, they just clock in and play good dog/bad coyote, and then they clock out. And then there was some movie, I don't think it was one of the "Oh, God" series, but maybe it was an episode on TV? At any rate, the theme of this skit was that God and the devil are just characters in a story and they play their parts just like Wiley Coyote and the Sheep Dog. So now you have the background of where my mind was at.

The episode in my life where the devil tried to choke me to death and sat on my chest was truly frightening. And I feel that it was brought on by my sympathetic (and VERY naïve) nature back then, being stimulated by the cartoons and movies of the day as described above. There were a handful of them in the 70s and 80s, setting the mood of the era, that bad people are just there to teach us a lesson, they can't choose for themselves.

Reinforcing this notion was a two hour debate which included jokes and laughter had between Uncle Lynn and un-alan, right there in the living room with all of the kids from both families present.

I felt him before I saw him, and didn't see him clearly anyway. It might've just been a ghostly asshole of the male persuasion – heck if I know for certain. Maybe he had followed me from that spooky house on State Street in Clearfield. We had just moved in from there.

But I decided I felt sorry for him and told him I would be his substitute mom and love him since no one else had, according to the mormons. (And the people who stole me from my momma were mormons.) They believe the devil never got to have a body because of his rebellion against God in Heaven. To them, the War in the Heavens that's described by so many scriptural and historical accounts as an actual war Earthlings saw in the sky, is a fight that broke out in Paradise where God resides. As if he would even allow such nonsense.

So, in my foolish and naïve 13-year old mind, I thought I could change the world by showing love to the devil.

I think we should all stop and relieve the building tension in our minds right here, and laugh at this foolishness.

You done? Okay.

Let me tell you, he doesn't care. He finds it humorous and sees us all as his inferiors.

Oh, sure, he might play along with you for about 5 minutes, complete with warm fuzzies, and then will suddenly try and steal your breath, hands on your throat and sitting on your chest as you lie in your bed.

Again, I'm not entirely certain this was the actual evil one, but he was evil enough.

I was glad that I had practiced shallow breathing after hearing a radio theater character had been able to deceive her killer in that way and had survived. I had thought at 7 years old that might come in handy later, and practiced all the time. So here I was getting an opportunity to practice again. Can you feel my sarcasm?

It did. But I still got dizzy. I nearly blacked out – using my mind to call for God – and un-dad came in just in the nick of time and frightened this specter away. Which is weird by itself.

And when I told him about it he asked, "What did you learn?"

I blinked at him for a second. Then I murmured wryly, "I learned that the devil doesn't care."

And this man laughed like I'd just told a great joke.

And I just sat there looking at him with new eyes.

Now, I didn't perform a séance, light candles, draw out a pentagram or use an Ouija board. All I did was say what I said.

I did do one thing though, that tells me I knew how dangerous that might be, and that was to pray to God ahead of time, letting him know what I planned to try and do.

I wouldn't recommend any of you try this. I would just skip trying to give any evil spirit any kind of love to change their outlook. In fact, I would just skip ahead to the rebuking. It's the best solution to the problem of an unwanted spirit visitor.

When I said this prayer to God, he didn't warn me or try to stop me, but I believe he was observing somewhere close. And I think this was because he knew I had to find out for myself how foolish the world is to believe what I was taught by these stupid programs. Yes, the devil has a purpose by testing us, but he truly is evil and he does it because he hates us. Compassion cannot turn him, and he's not just clocking in and out for a job.

So don't try. That would be my advice after such an experience. Don't believe Hollywood and philosophers who say he's just a slug like us, clocking in and out daily.

What evil spirits need is an ass whipping, and a time out in outer darkness.

My Bird Died

Sunny, who had survived a stroke when my brother's had chased her up and down the hall in Grandma Kathy's house, and limped on her perch with one club foot, finally died. She made it 5 years past the normal parakeet life span.

I went through all 7 stages of grief that summer – but really rapidly. Which got me musing again about my take on life and death.

I had a yellow recipe card file that had toll painting on it in a red tulip motif and thought that would be the most appropriate coffin for her. I made her a little pillow and cushion and blanket. I put a little bell-ball in there with her and cleaned her cage and put it back empty in my bedroom.

For several days after I buried her under a tree in our yard, I would sit out her tiny grave and just ache to have her back.

And at least twice she came to visit and perched in the tree above me. But because she was in her spirit form and tiny and translucent, I didn't notice her at first until she'd flitted about a little. I nearly mistook her each time for a little patch of buttery sunlight.

Each time she would finally get my attention, we would just look at each other for a few seconds and then she would flit away, flying over my head where I sat and giving a quick chirp.

My First Of Many Nirvana Experiences.

When we moved into the Shumway's cottage house in town, I was told I would be sleeping in the basement, until I wheedled my way out of it.

I could feel, and sometimes see a very angry looking guy in his 40s down there, and there were spiders, which I wasn't really scared of, but didn't want the spider bite welts to go with my occasional pimples. Plus, the old furnace was right in the middle of the room and I kept worrying how far away from such a thing was safe to avoid catching the whole basement on fire with any of my belongings.

It also gave me flashbacks of the dirt cellar the house in Salt Lake City had sat directly on top of, and the two ghosts I had felt down there every time I was sent to fetch something.

I kept begging for the tiny sapphire blue room upstairs at the back of the house, but it and the adjoining bedroom were given to my brothers.

So I was given the other upstairs bedroom and my imposter parents said they'd sleep on the couches in the living room. (Honestly, I would've been fine if that went the other way around.)

What really ended up happening was I was told to sleep on the floor in the closet because they needed some sexy time on the bed. And I would hear them making love and get super embarrassed.

More than once they offered to let me climb into the bed with them but I always refused each time, because gross! And I was 13 now. That is way too old to be climbing into bed with your parents and would seem kinda' perverted to anyone finding that out. Even if nothing happened. But this is un-alan we're talking about, so you and I both know at this point that *something* would likely happen. So no.

One of these nights, I knew I had tests the next day in several of my classes in middle school and was under so much pressure to get a good grade. I couldn't sleep because of this and kept staring at the ceiling, seeing that dark cloud of chi begin forming and roll over onto my stomach putting my hands palms up to cradle my head. I kept praying and praying and praying.

About everything. About my family relationships that were anxiety causing and how awkward I felt with my friends and about the boys I had a crush on and how I wished I could have my own bedroom that didn't feel like a death trap or a nightly haunting session. If my mind had actual gears, there would've been smoke.

All of a sudden I started to feel like I was on Earth on the floor in my bedroll and up in the stars over the planet at the same time. Rapidly switching back and forth. Then it expanded to where I could feel the skin of the entire universe, like a golden balloon made of energy, glittering. And then the next millisecond I was a tiny grain of energy the size of a grain of sand. And this would shift back and forth and back and forth and was almost frightening.

I asked God, "What is this? What's happening? Am I dying?"

I heard a very faint murmur, "Well, you're breathing."

"Oh."

And just like when someone tries to hypnotize me, I started focusing on each phase of what I was experiencing. Gradually, one gets used to it and it just feels like a steady, tingly, numbness in the fringes of your energy bubble that surrounds you, and a tranquility like nothing else. Everything sparkles with this soft golden glowing and sparkles. Even with your eyes closed, it feels like you have never been more real than in that moment. You are aware of everything around you – house, furnishings, neighborhood. And yet, you somehow feel like they aren't there at the same time.

I went from being afraid of this feeling, to loving it.

It wasn't until I was working in a law office in California and one of the clients somehow dragged us both into this crazy conversation about yoga, meditation and unusual experiences. So I told him about this little cycle I could get into when I prayed and focused long enough.

"Nirvana?!" He was incredulous. "You've experienced Nirvana already?!"

I asked, "Is that what that is?"

"Yes." He was annoyed and jealous, he told me. He was older than me and he wanted to know how I got there. So I described it again while typing away, flipping through folders, checking my lists.

Then he had me write it down. He wanted step by step instructions.

All I could do was write on a post-it that he needed to focus on everything in his life that concerns him right now and reach out to God.

And I do mean, reach OUT – waaaaaaaaaaaaaaaaaaaaaaaaaaaaaaay out. Out there into where you feel the furthest reaches of space are.

And there's this crazy thing your soul and your brain does that's kind of like you're made of bungee material.

And then I just described it as I did the first time. Like I did here in this entry.

Until you've experienced it, there isn't really any way to fully understand what I'm describing here. You really have to go on a mental and spiritual quest.

And yet, anyone can do it. I know you can.

My Friend Goh-tu

Okay, Cathy J. Quawpaw, as you requested, here goes:

So, the landlady owned the house that used to go with a garage (you could see the outline of the garage door around the living room window through the plaster) that had been turned into a mother-in-law house, but she divided the yard into two and rented out both separately.

They were both yellow with blue trim, and made me think of blue bonnet margarine, so that's what me and my kids call them to this day, the blue bonnet houses.

We were living in the mother-in-law house. It was tiny: living room with these cute French doors, kitchen, one bath, an upstairs bedroom and then in the basement (yes, it had been given a basement) was just one big multi-purpose room with 2 closets, neither had doors on them. One was the washer and dryer nook. The other was the clothes closet. My youngest two slept there in that room, the other two were grown and out on their own.

Next to the nook was a door into a very skinny hallway where the furnace and water heater were, and you could see where there used to be a way to the other house, a bricked in tunnel.

The wall behind the other closet wasn't finished – the cinderblocks only came halfway up, and it was piled up with garbage and dirt and broken furnishings on the other side of the wall. I could never tell where the back of the opening was.

You could go over it if you wanted, but it was creepy and dark. I didn't have the nerve to shine a flashlight into it even. I could feel someone or something hanging out there.

Our first night in there, we were still without my bed and living room furniture, so I made a little bedroll and lay there watching Netflix. (Wood floors throughout the upstairs added to the quaint hominess.)

I sort of started to sleep, but not quite, and I see this man, kind of reminded me of a mummy, with his skin shrunk around the bones, wearing a ragged yellow loincloth, short black hair,……starts walking towards me from the corner of the kitchen by the back door, but a little off the floor, then drifts into a kneeling position next to my head on the pillow, and he starts talking to me in a deep, growling voice.

When I squint I can see him, when I open my eyes I can't, can't hear him either. So I do that squinting into the sun thing.

I can't make out the words, new language for me. But his tone I don't like.

I sit up into a cross-legged position, point in front of me into his chest and push him back and push him back and up as I stand, then backwards to the back door the way he came, open the door and push him outside.

Then I shout, "Get out of my house and don't come back in if you're going to act like that! This is my house now, you're dead!"

Then I slammed the door.

He came back later, but he would only pinch our ribs. Especially my youngest when he would backtalk me and not do his schoolwork.

My youngest told me about it once, and I got mad and walked to the back steps and shouted down to the basement, "Are you pinching my son?!"

And then I hear, "Shhhhhh." (Like he's trying to say, "Lady, calm down.")

I whip around to see him sitting on the floor crosslegged, next to my stove.

"Did you just tell me to shush in my own kitchen!"

He looked embarrassed and faded away like steam.

The weirdest thing I kept noticing about him was that I could see his teeth through his lips, like a mummy, you know?

Well, my daughter would bring my grandson, who was 2, over to my house and have him stay the night cuz of her work schedule. Sometimes he'd be at my home for several days.

He would always scoot on his butt down the cement stairs, but walking up, no problem.

One afternoon I was having a discussion with my youngest from the top of the stairs, and my grandson was next to him on the other side next to the railing.

Suddenly, he jumps sideways in fear, shouts, "Ah, ZOMBIE!", then runs UP those stairs so fast it was like he was a little cartoon character. (He was 2, remember.)

Every time I tell this part it makes me laugh, seeing that in my mind again. Just a minute.

LOL

I get this chill down my back and arms, and my youngest looks at us from the bottom of the stairs like, "what?" This kind of thing kept happening and I kept trying to find out what kind of ghost it was.

Well, there was an episode of T.A.P.S. where they paired up with some other ghost hunters and go to Guam. They tell about the Guam Zombie (Tautaumono) which are ancient ancestors of the islands there, and how they will pinch kids who don't mind their parents and are rude. And not to touch those banyan trees which are sacred, or one of them will follow you home.

I'm like, oh! That looks a lot like him. And there's the pinching. Maybe some idiot brought some of that banyan wood? Or climbed a tree on vacation?

We stayed at that house 1 ½ years, until I noticed the gas bill had doubled, called the gas company, and the technician they sent out right away turns off the gas after showing me the blower was sending the flames backwards. Clogged.

I tell him how the landlady had just took the red tape off the valve while showing me the house and turned it back on. He was putting more red tape on it and looked at me and said, "That's a violation."

So, we're already planning to move after that, cuz we have no heat and no stove because of this. But the next morning, I wake up to my answering machine turning on and off repeatedly. "To set the date and time".....click, click, "To set the date and time", etc.

I'm thinking it's my grandson playing with the power strip button. But just then he comes running in, "Bubbe, come look!"

So I follow him into the living room, and it's doing this by itself.

Then I hear a tiny crackle sound, and then I go over to the stairs where the power panel is, and see that it's arcing with hair-like strands of blue electricity.

I'm like, "Oh, crap!"

The wiring for this garage —a – la- house, is that old kind with the black cloth insulation.

I put two and two together and tell the boys, "We are packing up this house into the garage, (yes, there was an additional garage we rented), and we are going to stay at your sister's until we get a place."

I turned the power panel off too, cuz it wouldn't stop arcing.

(It's a miracle those two houses haven't burned down, unless the landlady got wise and had them rewired.)

When we were done packing and cleaning, I stood at the stairs and said, "Hey, thank you. I didn't know you were trying to save our lives."

A couple of weeks later at the new apartment, I hear an old man with a deep voice singing his death song.

I'm like, "What?"

I keep looking out my back window to the grass and see nothing, then I hear him again, 3 more times. Then it's quiet, and I hear this beautiful woman's voice say, "Goh-tu is leaving now, he wanted to say goodbye."

And then I start crying those happy tears, like when a baby is born, or the sunset is so beautiful you can't stand it. And I say, "Thank you, God, for this experience. Thank you we could be his good deed so he could leave here."

The next day I sang that song that goes, "Wen-deh-yah-ho, wen-deh-yah-ho....." which I should probably sing every morning, but I forget.

And then a few weeks later someone tells me that this town used to be a Ute village, the kind with the houses sunk into the ground – dugouts? – cuz they're easier to keep the right temperature. And that the miners when they moved in and found the places abandoned kept a lot of these dugout places and turned them into tunnels to go between the houses in the winter, and to help black people hide during the Civil War.

(I know, you're not supposed to even touch the pot shards in such a place, but how would these German and Scandinavian immigrants know that? They were still learning English.)

I mean, this town is so haunted it should be a series on t.v. Maybe I should tell you what happened to me in the old Safeway next.

So, needless to say, I don't think the old guy was a Tautaumono, with the Death Song and all, that's local customs.

But does anyone know a story about a guy named Goh-tu?

My Grandma Helen Looks Out For Me

The very best thing in Grandma Helen's living room - to me - was the piano.

When my brothers were still in diapers, Mike had used the music holder to climb up on the bench and bent one of it's hinges, and partially tore out it's screws. Yet Grandma, who always kept everything in good repair, never had it repaired. For the memories?

The brother underneath him, Brian, accidentally dropped the wishbone piece from the game "Operation" into the back where the wires were. And I had famously left my Sunday School papers I got when attending church with Grandma in the bench with the music. I say famously, because this kept coming up, and everyone knew that I kept forgetting to take them home with me. And the worst earmark of all on this beautiful instrument was my mistake of getting cranberry fingernail polish on the seat. Grandma never removed it. These are the tagging that let me know later I had this very piano, as you will see.

Many years later (2000), I was cut out of any inheritance at all – just items, not money. I was very hurt about it. I hadn't yet realized that Helen wasn't my DNA grandma.

To make matters worse, I had been told that I couldn't have the piano because one of the aunts might want it, but neither one did.

Yet my imposter parents, who had somehow finagled their way back into residence in that beautiful red brick home on the corner, refused to even let me come and get it. Not even if I bought it from them.

They sold it to outsiders!

Worse yet, these outsiders had some trouble lifting it down the short three steps of the front porch to their pickup truck, and one of the ornamental legs (meant to be removed and set aside while moving it) popped off, and my imposter father stupidly screwed it back on with a woodscrew and a drill!

And then he made sure to call me and tell me all about it, pretending to have forgotten that I had asked for the piano.

This piano ended up here in Colorado in this little town, even after the foreclosure on that family's home.

And then appeared in the flier pinned up by the Mennonites.

The only other thing I'd wanted was one of her old fashioned hairpins she made those little curls by her temples with, 1920s style. I wanted one because of my memories of standing in the bathroom doorway while she curled her wet hair up with those on either side before going to bed. It was the first memory of her that popped into my head when they called me to tell me she had passed on.

The pettiness of refusing to even take one of those and drop it in an envelope with some postage and send it to me should give you some idea of my status in that family.

Why even bother asking me if there's anything I want from her? But this kind of cruelty was their favorite hobby.

So about a decade later when I had moved to another state, I saw a flier pinned up on the community bulletin board in the mall and was shocked to see a maple colored Emerson upright piano "for sale or trade", posted by some Mennonites.

I went and looked at the piano, sitting in their attached garage, made a trade for my nearly new washing machine I couldn't hook up in my apartment,(I had moved from a house), and waited for the delivery by 8 Mennonite guys. I was truly impressed. 8 of them, 4 on each side, all the way up the 3 flights of stairs to my apartment! So amazing!

The washer was quite a bit easier for them and they only needed 2 guys for it, but they were all smiles because their washer had just broken.

As I sat down to play it for the first time, I noted the nail polish on the seat, the broken hinge on the music holder, and the missing knob on the keyboard cover that my youngest brother of 3 had unscrewed and lost. Forgot to tell you about that one.

As I discovered my Sunday School handouts and some beginner books for piano in the bench, I realized that God and Grandma had made certain that I would get that piano.

The wishbone piece from the Operation game wouldn't fall out until we had moved the piano from Colorado to Washington and back to Colorado again, reminding me of the miraculous way this piano became mine.

That little piece of white plastic is like a little note from my grandma. I am trying to figure out how I want to wear it as jewelry.

Sometimes the ghost is a relative, and they are looking out for you.

Peeping-Tom Artist

Shortly after "Witness" was born and swapped with "Mickey", I was nursing Mickey in the wee hours of the morning, and felt eyes on me.

I looked up just in time to see a head move back quickly.

It was so quick, and so dark out, I couldn't even tell what color the skin was on this person. By the time I put my eyes on their forehead, it had taken on that bluish grey tone the moonlight gives everything until your eyes adjust fully.

It's just too much like what happened when I had been nursing "Nikko-kun" 7 years ago.

So I shared this with a friend I had until she moved – I lose so many friends to moving – and she mentioned what I was thinking. There has to be one common person planning all this. It's like a signature. All the same things keep happening to me.

It was either the next day or within a few days of this that I was pushing Mickey around the neighborhood in his stroller and went down the next street from ours, only to see a pencil sketch of me nursing Mickey in someone's window facing the street! It was almost photo quality. Particularly the moment when I rubbed my cheek against his soft, baby-fuzz hair! Which is when I saw that forehead.

I was so unnerved by it, I didn't have the courage to find out who lived there. I knew this was who had been looking in my window, though.

You can bet I made sure my curtains and blinds were all the way closed at night after that.

Like I said, this had happened once 7 years ago, catching someone watching me nurse Nikko-kun, there was no pencil sketch the first time, though. And now again with Mickey. To you it's just a coincidence, but to me it's something I should've already learned to safeguard against. Why had I been so foolish?

I kept wondering who lived there without the nerve to go back and knock.

Pneumonaultramicroscopicsilicavolcanoconiosis

Yeah, it's a real word, which is a lung disease one gets from exploring around a volcanic crater too much without a mask.

Nowadays they just call it Pneumonosis.

It was a spelling word I had used to spell the longest word in the dictionary in Mr. Sheinberg's class. And I won.

But there's this thing with frequently repeating something in thought and speech and attracting it to you. It's one of the main tools in the Law of Attraction for manifestation.

Now I'm not saying that I made Mount Saint Helen's erupt, but on May 18, 1980, after repeatedly using this word as a conversation piece and showing off over the previous 2 years with anyone who would let me, this happened.

And then I got a mild case of pneumonaultramicroscopicsilicavolcanoconiosis. Because rectangles of ash blew all the way out to Thermopolis and fluttered down onto our town. There was a good inch thick layer of ash on our family car, the sidewalk, grass, leaves on the tree out front, everything.

And I was out playing in it, breathing it and catching these rectangles of ash thinking they reminded me an awful lot of plant cells when magnified.

Elaine kept screaming from all of us kids to come inside, and the boys did. But I kept saying, "This is science." And, "These are the same size and shape as a stick of gum, but look at this! It smears on my fingertips."

Finally Elaine screeched at me, "Get inside! The newscaster said to stay inside because that's Mount Saint Helen's ashes, it erupted. It's not good for your skin! Get in here!"

So, did I make this happen by repeating the word and wishing I could go study the volcanoes in Hawaii? Or is it a coincidence. LOL

Even if it's a coincidence, on some level I manifested pneumonaultramicroscopicsilicavolcanoconiosis into my life.

Safeway Ghost

I had a very frustrating two months working as a cashier at Safeway here in this cottage town. There were managers and other administrative personnel breaking the rules – and sometimes the law – and making the new cashiers take the fall for it one at a time.

When you were the newest cashier, no one messed with you and they were really friendly. When you were the second newest they would start harassing you while you were eating lunch and imply you had stolen it, even though I always brought my food in my own Tupperware and made it ahead of time at home. I watched this happen to the person ahead of me. When you were the one there the longest – which would be the third cashier, they would frame you to make it look like you had stolen money from your till and shoplifted the very things that the head cashier and the produce manager were stealing out the back door - which was broken in such a way that it would look secured, but if you spanked it hard enough it would pop wide open.

I watched the guys in receiving do this a couple of times when they had locked it and the key was inside. And I saw this while walking home to my apartments behind the store and the mall.

I found this routine by the head cashier and her produce manager buddy very despicable. The average amount of time before the police were called and you were handcuffed and taken away was about 3 months. One month for each stage of this process. I saw this happen on my first day to a 4th cashier who was then no longer there of course.

During my first month, I watched this happen to the one who was on the 3rd register. And I watched this begin to happen to the 2nd cashier as I became the 2nd cashier and she became the 3rd cashier. And also, I suddenly went from having a perfectly zeroed out register to having a few cents over or under, and then a dollar and some change short, and it was steadily increasing a few cents at a time per shift. I knew by now what the pattern was and I refused to be the next victim.

I also was subjected to the head cashier using her manager's discount card, plus several coupons off (which is against the rule and is like stealing) and this was done to two full grocery carts of food each week. She worked this so the total owed was between $20-50 per combined purchase on what was probably $500 or more of food and other items! And then she would use some of her food stamps. And she did all this in my checkout line. I knew if I said no, I would have problems.

I also watched her buddy who managed produce slide trays of meat, various veggies and other things into her extremely deep pockets on her Aladdin-style pants, more than one time. She was overweight and thought she was fooling people this way. But more than one employee saw her doing this. Sometimes she would even go out the front door. But mostly she would clock out and go through the back door in receiving. Outright theft on her part. There's no telling how much she stuffed into those huge pockets that went nearly down to the bottom of the pant legs. Later I was told by one of the produce guys that they finally got disgusted enough they called the police together.

Anyway, like I said, I quit. I didn't appreciate where they were trying to steer my life without my consent.

I went on with my life and took a couple of temp jobs in neighboring towns and then found an ad for a security position which required a week training Colorado Springs. Hotel and food paid for except dinner. I had a couple of years of security experience and applied, got hired and got a surprise. My assignment was to provide security for the contractors disassembling our Safeway grocery store.

I thought it very poetic that the name of the security company was the very same name as the one found in the Girl With The Dragon Tattoo novel.

Now when I first reported for duty, the store was still open and wrapping things up, selling their inventory out. Everyone on staff was pretty friendly with me, but the head cashier saw my face and freaked out. Hilarious! I still laugh thinking about it. She was in such a panic and trying to get me fired by within my first 10 minutes on the clock, by telling all kinds of things to the interim GM, right in front of me!

Some of the things she said were so wild, I just tilted my head sideways and watched. I couldn't not watch. It was like pulling up to an intersection and seeing a collision. I had to stand there anyway and observe the cashiers and the customers for a little while until there was no one going through with their purchases. Then I would wander the store and then the parking lot and then it was back to the registers if they were full. I knew my job. Observe and report.

The cashier obviously thought I was in more authority and that I would get revenge. I'm laughing again while I type this.

A few minutes later after the GM curtly told her to go do her job, he sauntered over to me and told me she was saying all kinds of things about me being a safety risk and I shouldn't have a gun.

I looked at him and blinked. I think I might have even done that mouth agape thing like that little girl in the meme. I had heard some crazy stuff coming out of her mouth, but I hadn't overheard that. I was actually doing my job and paying attention to the activity at the registers.

When he was done telling me, I laughed out loud. "She's just paranoid because she did me very wrong as a cashier and thinks I'm here for revenge." I couldn't quit laughing, but I kept the volume down.

He looked at me with a twinkle in his eye and smiled. "I also noticed you don't have a gun." Then he chuckled.

"Well, that's because this is an unarmed position, right?" I kept giggling quietly.

Then we both shrugged and smiled at each other and went back to our work.

That goofy female only had a week to go on the job anyway, and then I would be guarding a locked building at night while the demo-crew took it all down. Including the shelves, freezers, everything. Besides that, I was the only one in the store after about 6 or 7 pm, depending on the day for the crew.

I was the graveyard shift.

One night while walking my rounds I decided to mix it up a little and go up to the office and check out some odd sounds I'd heard.

Now, there is only one way up and down from there, the staircase. This staircase travels up from the area near the registers and I was pretty sure no one had found a way to sneak in there. And I was mentally prepared to run like the wind if there was someone up there.

I wasn't prepared to find a very tall woman, native, with long black hair, in full regalia. Nor was I prepared for her to be translucent and incredibly angry. Safeway had a ghost? What? I just stood there looking at her for a minute or so. Why would a native woman's ghost be in the office inside Safeway?

Again, I found myself with that facial expression, blinking and mouth agape. I think it might have been the second time in the same week.

I sighed heavily, turned around and speed walked to the stairs, feeling her anger right at my back, complete with static.

"Hey," I said calmly, "I don't know how long ago this happened to you, but I didn't do it. It's the year 2013. Probably has been more than 100 years since this was done to you. Whatever it was. And I'm part Tsalagi, so come on. Give me a break." I had come to a halt by now and still had about twelve feet to go before the stairs.

The static subsided, and I turned to see her as nothing more than a grey shape. "Good night," I said softly. Then I went down the stairs.

I didn't go back up there for several days. Let her calm down before I go walking around up there. Besides, it might not be her regular haunt. Who knows.

I never saw her again after that, but sometimes I felt her there. Nothing really very frightening about her, just startling. Well, for me. Should you run into her, it might be a different experience.

Big O Tires is in there now, I wonder if any of them has encountered this woman.

Snowmist Warriors

Here's another Utah chiller:

I'm forced to bring a load through Utah by my freight company, Warner.

(Let me catch you up; C. R. England was not putting me on a trainer truck after about 2 months because I insisted on a female trainer, and kept sending me male trainers which I rejected. So I had snuck out of CRE at 2 am on a friend's trainer truck after Werner hired me over the phone.)

Anyway, I'm done training, have my own truck now, and there's this load. Through Utah. Don't go there, that place is unclean. As in unclean spirits, dirty deals, child sex traffickers frequent there, drugs, drug deals, polygamy, and any other kind of weird and creepy dangerous stuff you can imagine. Dirty energy. It's unclean.

I'm coming through Heber, and I see the most bizarre formation in this meadow off in the distance, looks like snow, but vaporized like fog. Shadows like braves on horses with spears, but kind of giant sized. White shadows.

I start slowing down, cuz I get that rush of heat to my cheeks like when you might black out. I take the offramp and sit there on the shoulder, trying to not hyperventilate.

I'm not usually like this when I see a ghost, especially a native ghost. But this is a war party. I can tell they're angry, vengeful.

I calm myself down, tell myself I'm being silly, then cross over to the onramp directly across from the offramp and keep truckin'.

A few seconds later, I see them again.

Let me describe this better: I see the green meadow, then this white fog feathers and swirls like a fog is known to do,(but looking heavy like snowmist), and then it rises up all 3D like, and I'm seeing a war party all white made from this heavy fog, giant sized (like how it sometimes looked on 9/11 as if people's faces were enlarged in the smoke), spears, feathers, bonnets and all. Made of this weird fog.

I pull off again at the next offramp. Repeat the process from before, get back up there on the highway – it happens again.

There's other rigs ahead of me that I can see now, and as they follow the curve and go up the hill, this war party starts charging at each one, lifting their back wheels of their trailers off the ground, and nearly tipping the whole rig.

They each right themselves and keep driving.

I get closer to the spot, and I keep watching over my shoulder, and in my mirror.

I see them rise up again just before I can't look out my driver's side window to see them and – I swear to God – I make eye contact with 3 of them one at a time, I felt their consciousness, and then the whole party came at the back of my truck. (8 or 9 of these giant things.)

I see my tandems at the very back of my trailer through my mirror lift at least 12 inches, maybe more, and I am FULLY loaded to 60K! (Max is 80K, but the load was something light, can't remember what.)

I feel that panicky gulp in my larynx, and I start yelling, "Hey, I'm Tsalagi! I'm not one of them Mormon bastards that killed you! Hey, stop it!"

I yelled this cuz they kept lifting the wheels.

They stopped, but the wind that came with them kept blowing forcefully, and then it started to rain pretty heavy, with little hail balls mixed in. The tiny ones.

I see an independent truck stop and decide to accept the omen to stop. I call in, tell them what happened (not the ghostly snowmist, just the weather part) and that I only have 45 minutes drive time left anyway.

I say, "I am still shaking, I can't drive right now."

I pulled in, got dinner and a shower and pulled out early the next morning.

But like I said, I HATE Utah.

That Place Is Unclean

Every time it was Sabbath and we were out and about, if there were any mormon men around – especially the older ones - we would get the dirtiest looks and anti-semitic comments.

Plus, Mickey looks Hispanic. And the things they said about him and our mixed family made it possible to believe my former babysitters who were Hispanic, back before I had Mickey. Utahns are very racist. They mask it well in most cases, but they are racist. Especially the priesthood holders. Evidently, when you kids are all blonds because their dad is of Norwegian descent, you can camouflage if you have blue eyes, even if your skin is a little dark. Not so if one of your kids is brown. Game changer for me.

The only jobs I could get were a temp job at a weird factory, a job at the factory where they made window shades, and a job at a call center.

While at this job, there was this soon-to-be missionary for the mormon cult who found out I was Jewish and wouldn't leave me alone any time he found me in the break room.

It was even worse to be sitting by my ex-husbands current wife during training. She wasn't as fat as she had been while screaming at me in Virginia in front of the police station, and she wore a nametag that had her last name as Baker. I guess I'm supposed to use my psychic skills 24/7? No.

She starts asking questions about whether I'm married or not. I show her my hand, "See, no wedding ring."

Then we start having discussions about obnoxious husbands and I tell her things about my ex which I would not have had I known or recognized her at that time. I told her about when Fred had tried to smother me and dislocated my jaw, about the sexual abuse of the kids by him, and about catching Fred and Harry kissing on my couch, shirts off. Well, now she knows.

I caught my imposter parents leaving the parking lot some time later in their gold 4 door sedan and they giggled and avoided my gaze. They had told my boss that I wasn't born Jewish. Jokes on them, my real mom was

Jewish before I was born. That means I was born Jewish. But in mormon land, this is not a good thing to have known, that you were raised amongst them and have attended their services and such. I lost Sabbath day off that day, and Liar-lyn and she were tete-a-tete all shift.

I tried to complain about the missionary nonsense on my breaks from this kid I told you about earlier, but to no avail.

I applied for a transfer to the facility in Colorado, this supervisor blocked me.

I came up to negotiate with her for my Sabbaths off, and found her telling this missionary kid not to worry about getting into any trouble because she was a "straight edger" and she was mad at me for my heresy. As if. To be a heretic, one must still be a participant, and I had resigned my membership and now told people "I'm not a mormon." I never really was. When you read my memoirs you'll understand.

I looked up "straight edger" and found out it's a mormon gang, known for their vicious attacks on unbelievers.

And then I called my imposter parents and discussed the whole thing with un-dad.

"Don't worry about that. In General Conference one of the General Authorities spoke about church gangs and told people they are akin to secret societies and God doesn't approve."

I pursed my lips and nodded my head silently. "Ah, that's good. Dad – what about the Danites?" (this group is the long arm of the mormon president/prophet)

Dead silence, muffled fuming. And after that phone call he wouldn't talk to me for at least a decade.

Perfect excuse to not call anymore.

I quit this job soon after because of all this stupid drama.

But during the next couple of weeks some really odd and scary things happened.

First, we had discovered that the Great Salt Lake – an ancient super volcano – had awoken. The previous summer Sha-sha had taken pictures while on a field trip with her school class of steam coming up from a crevice in the dirt on the point of Antelope Island. Which at that point had become a peninsula because the water had been evaporating. The orange algae and brine shrimp were gone. The snow had continued to melt to nothing around the lake, when in the years I had visited there while growing up the shore had been buried under a thick blanket of snow until spring every year. Scary.

The woman at the film developers told us that most of the role of film had been heat and moisture damaged. So I told her what my daughter told me. Her face showed what I was thinking and we had a little discussion about leaving before it was too late.

I went to the library and found Antelope Island on Google Earth. There was a lovely little orange circle at it's base in that little bay on the floor of the lake. I zoomed out next, and sucked in air. All of the peaks around this huge lake were really connected into a perfect circle. The lake was a huge crater.

Time to move again. Needed to wait for tax season and the refund.

While studying Torah next, God said to me, "Tell your people. Then move."

My people? The Jews have never acknowledged me. I can't claim my native heritage because my imposter father refused to go get my number in 1972 in North Carolina after making a trip to the Western band and they didn't know who I was. If he had gone Eastern band, my mom had prepared some paperwork and left it with someone there I found out later. I don't think this can be fixed at this point. My real family, the Dylans, all act like I'm some kind of monster thanks to Shirley. She has all kinds of stories of things I've never said or done. The mormons are definitely not my people. They have always treated me badly and anyway, I'm really not one of them, since birth. And my imposter family had cut me off. Like Fiddler on the Roof. (Mormons claim they are the new Israel.)

I had already told my kids. What people was God talking about? I kept asking him.

Should I try and warn the nation? Via USGS? I tried, and boy did I get ridiculed.

So I kept asking God. Silence, or so it seemed. So I told all the groups I thought of, USGS, my neighbors in the apartment complex, even my imposter family. I hadn't yet figured out who my real dad was, so I only tried to contact my real siblings from my real mom. The Jewish Congregants I worshipped with at both temples.

I kept getting made fun of. "Okay, look, God," I huffed, "I have tried. I don't know who my people are anymore. If I've missed somebody I need you to tell me."

And I and the kids started packing up the house to get ready for California.

The second thing that happened was my door locks would keep clicking. They were manual, not electric. It sounded like Morse code, but it seemed to be all vowels. I'm not really great at Morse code. There were some messages about moving though.

One evening when I was on my way in to work the nightshift, this fireball as big a softball flew up next to my car and paced me for a little bit until it overcame my speed and then shot off down the highway and disappeared. That was in the news later. There were a few of those. This happened after the ground had shook enough I felt it in the car I was driving. The volcano was trying to erupt.

But this was the weirdest thing of all: the Grasshopper Man.

As I was coming home in the wee hours, I saw it. Spooky.

And I had just been told about these by a coworker who was also not a mormon. He was a catholic from Guatemala. I had heard brief discussion here and there in Virginia about sightings by coworkers there, but it hadn't been my conversation, so I left it alone and just wondered what they were.

But this guy met me at the coffee maker and asked me if I'd seen these things and described them to me. 6 to 7 feet tall and with backwards bending knees, but with flesh colored like a human and with a human looking face.

"So that's what those are. I thought I saw something out of the corner of my eye a few times driving back to Layton near that motel, but I thought maybe my mind was playing tricks on me from being tired."

"No, they are real! I almost got attacked by one. If you see them, you're not supposed to try and talk to them. Just look straight ahead and keep driving."

"Okay. Good to know."

And wouldn't you know it, he jinxed me!

I saw one of those creatures *that night,* talking to what looked to be regular people, but he wasn't attacking any of them. There were 3 humans with him. And as soon as I assessed that, he noticed me looking and we made eye contact for a second and he smiled. It seemed like a friendly smile. But I remembered what that coworker said and I wasn't taking any chances.

I punched the gas hard! And that thing sprung after me, jumping! By the time I reached 80 he lagged back. But I could still see him standing near the chainlink fence near the motel until I whipped around the bend. I don't think I encountered a skinwalker, but those things live down around that ranch there.

I'm gonna tell you again, don't go to the state of Utah. That place is unclean.

The Dark Mass Of Energy

One summer night, right before we moved to the "fancy crackerbox" in yet another part of Orem, I awoke suddenly to pitch blackness and ominous silence. And that bedroom was mostly just sad when the she-ghost was there, but she never gave off an ominous vibe. And even though I only had a smallish basement window, it was never pitch black in there, and even if it was, I have night vision. So this inky blackness was bad.

The terror.

And then I needed to pee so bad I thought I might leak before I could get off my bed to the door.

The black mass was hovering near my closet with little whispies waving around it. It was somehow darker than the rest of the room. And as long as I stayed on the bed it held still where it was. But each time I uncrossed my legs to put my feet on the floor, it slowly reached out and I can feel the dirty energy try to caress my feet. So I keep drawing them back in.

Finally, when I'm starting to get that floating teeth feeling, I decide that whatever it is, I don't have time to wait or I am going to pee all over the bed.

"Oh, grrrrrrrr! I have to pee!" I shout and make a mad dash for my closed bedroom door, feeling more than seeing the knob because of how unusually dark it was. And then I pulled the door shut behind me like I was locking that thing in there, trying not to stub my toes on anything as I hurry through the family room, into the hallway and then for the toilet before I end up having to change my underwear.

The whole time I'm praying for help. I do that now. God is my friend. Deal with it.

It must have just drifted through the closet and to the hallway, and then the bathroom. This thing kept fluffing at my arms, legs, face, and back while I sat on the toilet, and I finally growled, "Cut it out! I have to pee!!" It did, it stopped bothering me, and I even heard muffled male laughter in this mass. Seriously, why?

My night vision is pretty good, like I've said. I noticed that the trickle of moonlight slowly began to make it's way around the basement bathroom after I said that. I could see my feet pretty clearly again, and the orange, brown and yellow patches of color on the carpet became distinctive again.

I stood outside my room after relieving myself, but could not go in there, I could feel it still in there. And looking over to the couch in the family room, it didn't seem far enough away from my room. So I crept into my little brother's room and curled up on the bottom corner of his bed so I wouldn't be by myself. I was shook.

How did dad know to come down the stairs at just that moment and turn the light on in my brother's room, ignoring mine?

This is the type of thing he does that makes me feel that if anyone in that family is possessed, it's him, and maybe the dark mass of energy regularly takes up space in his body. Don't know for certain, but I feel it's highly likely.

He had come down the entire staircase, creaking and popping those old stairs as he went, so he certainly wasn't already downstairs. How had he known?

I was so quiet, other than that growl of urgency. I didn't even flush when I was done, so as not to wake the household.

He yelled at me to go back to my own room, implying I was in there to do kinky stuff – his kind of maneuvers.

I argued that I was curled up at the foot of the bed because I just wanted to NOT go back in my room because there was something spooky in there.

He actually called me a liar.

I reminded him about my special talents.

He stopped speaking and his eyes went huge. My special abilities still scare this man. He insisted I go back in my room.

I gritted my teeth and opened the door, immediately turning my light on. And I waited.

As soon as I heard him snoring in the room above me, I grabbed one of my quilts and went to the couch in the family room. And yes, that light in my bedroom was left on still. The rest of the night. And as I shut the door, I stared at the area where that thing had been – and I could still feel it sending out static even though I couldn't see it.

I still got up before anyone else, as usual, even after experiencing something like that.

And from that day forward, I would no longer spend any amount of time alone with imposter Alan.

To this day, I wonder if he was tied to that black mass, and what or who it was.

The Devil Dog

I had been getting all my exes showing up in this little out of the way town. I mean, they're exes for a reason.

First my ex husband Fred getting nosy while he was here inviting my boys to their step brother's wedding in Arizona. Then this guy named JJ who I had almost married. Engagement pictures, ring, the whole nine yards. (He later followed me up to Montana! And that is a spooky tale, so that's next I guess.)

Then my youngest kid's father following me around the local fair with his girlfriend next to him, calling me a bitch. He's not from here. Works for the railroad.

Then the worst one, crazy man-baby. Had to kick him out by leaving him in Oregon at the casino hotel on the way back from my storage in Washington because he was pulling my hair, yelling out weird stuff about his father being in the CIA, and pulling a shoestring rope out of his backpack, saying he was gonna make me tie myself up. Yeah, that's the end for this relationship. Moved his mom in across the street from me! And then he starts sitting on their back porch that faces my house, sticks out to the side from their house. He mad-dogs me all day from there. At one point, he racked a handgun at me from behind my son's work truck he'd parked on the street and then ran away (holding the gun) when I stepped around the front of the truck to ask him, "Hey! Did you just rack that thing at me?!"

So I'm feeling smothered and irritated and really fed up. A little nervous, but mostly bitchy.

I pray about it, where should I go to for awhile? Then I'm talking to my boys who are still living at home, and saying, "I feel like I gotta' get out of here for a couple of months. But I don't know where to."

Then I hear one of my spirit guides murmur "Kalispell" in my ear. But we're still talking about this urge I have to leave, so I wrap up what I'm saying and wait for a response from my boys. And then the spirit guide says "Go to Kalispell" in my ear again.

"I guess I'm going to Kalispell. That's the second time someone just murmured in my ear."

My kids are used to this. They grew up knowing I am able to see and hear spirits from time to time.

So I load up my little red car, a 1994 Dodge Spirit that has seen better times. The wheels were (it fixed itself, but that's yet another story) pigeon-toed because it was in a roll over (somersault style), where it flipped 9 times end over end. This guy Martinez – 3 owners before me – went off the road coming back from Baggs, Wyoming. He was the spirit guardian of that car. Kept me out of all kinds of trouble and danger. Once, when I was saying something about how a certain thing was all that and then some, he whispered in my ear from the back seat, "Si, en todos!"

But this isn't about him, it's about the Devil Dog in the Kalispell Grand Hotel.

I made a new friend named Helen, and her daughter worked there for at the time. We'd go by to visit her at work before we'd go eat somewhere.

The basement is super creepy, and I felt a man watching me that I could only see out of the corner of my eye, never full on.

But the weirdest time we were there was the afternoon we went there to see Helen's daughter and she came quickly down the stairs. Looked a little scared. But tried to pretend everything was fine.

She did her paperwork, and then we were going to go outside to talk.

But right before we did, I see this huge dog walk up to the top of the stairs, eyes GLOWING, sort of a soft yellow and green kind of way. Like the two colors shifted a little and swirled. I looked up and smiled at him, thought maybe he was someone's pet and the sun was just bouncing off of his retinas. He just sighed and laid on his stomach and folded his paws over each other.

I hear Helen's daughter telling her about a ghost dog just then. "Look, mom, she sees it too!" I hear this from just inside the next room.

Helen comes over and looks up to where I'm looking, gets a nervous look on her face, I'm just smiling. I still think it's a pet of one of the guests. Then she looks back at me from the other side of the doorway like she thinks I'm nuts to just stand there, not even scared at all. "Come on!" she urges quietly.

So I follow her outside where we stand talking while her daughter lights a cigarette, shaking. Red-faced. Like she was holding her breath earlier. You know, so you don't make a sound?

Helen asks, "You don't know about the Devil Dog?"

I look at her. And then I realized the dog was a little transparent. And maybe he was a little high to the windows for that glow to be sunlight bouncing on retinas. I wasn't afraid still. He had laid down like a good puppy.

"Maybe we should go get our lunch," I suggested.

Helen laughed. "Yeah, let's go get lunch."

The Ghost At The Hot Springs Pools

One of the first things we did when we got to Thermopolis was to tour the two public pools filled by the hot springs, and also toured the hot springs themselves.

I keep remembering one of my uncles when he was teenager or 20-something being our amateur tour guide – but then I correct myself mid-thought because neither of these uncles was there that day.

But it may have been the ghost of my cousin Kae who died when I was 7 or 8. He was barely 19 when he died. Either way, he was a blond, 20-something looking male.

He and I would interact and un-Alan would say, "ooookaaaay, so here we have such and such (reading from each of the several brass plaques at each area of interest.

Un-Elaine would get a fearful look on her face and look from me to him and back again. I thought she was worried about me getting pregnant or something, which was a topic that came up more and more often in those years. I didn't realize I was the only one who could see this guy.

My three brothers looked dumbfounded the first couple of times as I was talking to this guy, and I thought they were just in awe of their sister's ability to pick up a guy. But after that, they would start giggling, teasing me and mocking what I was saying. In fact, each time I spoke with our "guide" or asked him anything, I think they thought I was joking around on un-dad.

At one point one of them asked why I kept interrupting and who was I talking to, and I told them it was our guide, dad's friend.

That got un-dad's attention and he said, "Where? Who?"

I answered, "Very funny, dad. He introduced himself in the beginning of our tour."

I pointed at our "guide". Un-dad waved at him – but his eyes didn't lock on. I thought there was some secret beef between them they were trying to ignore to remain upbeat.

It wasn't discussed amongst us, but I have a feeling I was conversing with a ghost. This has happened to me my whole life this time around. Sometimes I am unaware that others can't see or hear what I can. Other times I am and try to be non-chalant so no one will notice me responding to these souls.

After telling me about a big getting boiled in the hottest of the three springs, which is why they roped it off and didn't want anyone getting too close, and un-alan listening to our exchange – at least my half of the conversation – and then reading the plaque afterwards to find it almost said the same thing, our guide told me he had to go do other things on his schedule. "I'll see you later," he smiled and waved as he walked away across the street and down the hill. I smiled and waved back.

"Nice guy," I said quietly.

Un-Alan said, "He seems like a nice guy. I didn't notice him."

"Dad! He said he's your friend and he was standing right here next to us the whole time."

I really thought my whole family could see him when I was in the experience.

The Ghosts Of C.A.P.S.

There was so much energy friction at that place, it made my whole outfit get static cling every shift I worked there, and that's real.

It's a miracle that the entire Check-In didn't just fall into the dirt basement with all the weight they put on that ancient subfloor they never changed, first of all.

But there were a number of spirits of former residents (aka inmates) that were done in by either their roommates or the resident managers (aka guards) drifting around day and night. The place had been in operation since the 1940s I was told. And these kinds of tragedies are common in corrections facilities of all kinds. I would see a whispy white shape – human sized – dart around a corner or over my head from a bathroom or dodging out a door after I opened it for random inspections on many occasions.

To me this is unremarkable. Most of the planet is haunted from time to time; we've been born and died so many times in so many places.

The remarkable haunts are the ones you catch on camera, like that "pusher ghost" as the locals call him, who wears navy blue coveralls and sneaks up behind you to push you out into the street, down some stairs, onto the tracks, etcetera. I saw him walking between the little cottage that was used as an office for the facility and the front row of rooms one night just before midnight. But only the bottom of his legs and his black work boots were seen on camera.

I know that I'm not the only resident manager that has seen him. When I asked my trainer and his son-in-law about it, they both started quivering and their faces went pale. They played it back with worried looks on their faces. I think we watched that about 3 or 4 times.

I then got the whole collection of stories about this mean and hateful spirit. And I was told by Jim Walker, my trainer, that he thought it might be one resident in particular who was hung on his bunk in one of those horizontal configurations with a rope back in the 1980s.

Why do they call that a hanging these days? Doesn't a hanging require that the victim be *hanging* from something, rather than only being trussed up like a roping calf? It's a misuse of the word.

There's the single mother that used to live in the tiny theater that was on the lot. We used this building to store men's and women's clothing that our residents could pick through for their use, since they only came to us with the clothes on their backs, which were sometimes prison uniforms. The only thing I ever saw of her spirit was her shadow moving at the top of the stairs between the two doorways there. Just a glimpse.

But there were several female residents who were terrified of her and had seen her do some spooky maneuvers through that building and that end of the lot.

The scurrying in the basement when I had to check on my rounds could've just been insects or mice under that little office-house. It didn't really raise my hackles.

The one that unnerved me sometimes was the guy with the heavy boots that would walk unseen over the floor upstairs in that cottage. Mostly after you had gone into the basement. It sounded like some big man was walking heavily across the building, and it sounded real, like a living person. Every time I heard it I would approach the top of the stairs very quietly, holding my breath, turning the knob in slow motion so it wouldn't make a noise. And every time I would find absolutely no one in there after I slipped quietly into the main room. Of course, then I had to check each of the rooms branching off from it. Zilch. Nothing. Every time. I hate that.

When I had my slip and fall on the black ice in the courtyard, it was actually over very quickly, 30 seconds or so. And that's what you see on the cameras, too. I slip, one knee up, one leg straight, and then centrifugal force makes my spine whip my head back hard.

And I was aware of that happening. But what I experienced was very weird.

I felt myself fall, the world turned sideways, and suddenly I had this guy on top of me in a navy blue jumpsuit grabbing me by the shoulders, wrestling me to the ground and shoving me over the edge of what I thought was a cliff - I was scrabbling with rocks and dirt and twigs on this cliff, even feeling the grit of the tiny rocks and dirt getting under my fingernails, trying to make sure I didn't fall down into a river I saw in the moonlight far below me. And then suddenly I was back in the real world, feeling my head smack hard into the ice on the tarmac with a sort of mushy sound.

I laid there, scared to move because of the sound my head made when it hit. I almost laughed at myself when I involuntarily said very loudly, "Oh, God, oh, god, oh, god, oh, god, oh, god!" It seemed like an overreaction to my logical side. I was embarrassed even if no one else heard it. Nothing really hurt yet, and *that* was scary. I felt around my head with my hand for any blood or brains, nothing but ice.

Someone else heard it, one of the residents. It was after curfew, so he was bound by contract to not open his door, but he risked it. "Hawke? Are you okay?"

"Not exactly, I fell."

"Well go find Walker and have him take you to the hospital."

I rolled onto my side and groaned. Now everything hurt. Head, jaw, spine, ribs, hips, and all the muscle structure. " Fuck!"

He shut his door.

Why hadn't Walker come to help me up? I was right outside the guard door and definitely he had seen me fall on security cam.

Slowly I got up into a crouch, and then stood. It kind of felt like getting bucked off a horse.

As I opened the door, DiMaggio – the boss – and Walker were sitting there behind the counter, and neither of them would look me in the eye. "Do you need me to take you to the hospital?" DiMaggio asked me.

I thought about that for a few seconds. What if they said I couldn't work for awhile? I had only been there four months and I had responsibilities. "I don't think so. Let me take some aspirin and see how I feel in a few minutes."

I found a bottle of actual aspirin shaking out two of the tablets, looking at them and then saying, "Nope. This is a 4 aspirin headache," and shaking out two more of them. Then I weakly stood up and shuffled through the door of Check-In to the sink at the far side of the kitchen. I stooped to let my hand catch the stream of water and guzzle some into my mouth, and felt my jaw swing freely.

"Well, that's just great," I muttered, bending over to drink the water anyway, then tilting my head back to drop the aspirin into the little lake in my mouth. I swallowed and bent to drink some more so there would be plenty to protect my stomach from the aspirin.

Only when I stood upright again did I realize I was dizzy and needed to lean on the edge of the sink for a few minutes. I decided that I should probably not do this kind of rapid movement for awhile.

I shuffled back into the office.

DiMaggio asked me again if he should call an ambulance.

"Do I have insurance yet?"

"It's your call," he offered. "Workman's comp should cover it."

"Workman's comp won't take care of my embarrassment. I think I'll try and finish my shift. I only have about 3 hours left."

Walker and DiMaggio looked at each other.

"Okay," the boss said. I'll be back in the morning to type up the accident report. I have to do that."

I nodded feebly and then put my hand to my head. Nodding was not okay either at that moment.

"Let me take you to the hospital, I don't like the way you look at the moment. You don't look like you feel very good. I can cover your shift for you."

I was starting to really feel the agony welling up everywhere. "Could I maybe just clock out and go home?"

"If that's what you want to do. If you decide you need to have the hospital check you out, let me know so I can make sure Workman's Comp covers it."

"Okay."

The drive home was quiet and I went in to try and lay down, but didn't feel right. So I went into the living room and turned on Netflix and propped myself up. I was worried about lying down and I knew I had a concussion at least.

Turns out I had relocated my dislocated jaw, cracked my skull in several places, cracked 7 vertebrae, and popped both hips off my sacrum – which explained the sheer agony of climbing in and out of the van, sitting or standing, laying on either hip and going up and down stairs.

I did finally end up on Workman's Comp. But all the assertions I would get pins put in me and need a walker for the rest of my life turned out to be false. And part of that was because the hospital refused to x-ray more than just my neck. They didn't want to get stuck with an unpaid bill if my insurance didn't go through. I never had a physician examine any of the areas I made sure they knew were hurting.

Even with me acting tough because I'm Gen-X and that's how I was raised, medical professionals have an obligation to thoroughly examine a person.

I guess there are some advantages to having a protein-S deficiency after all. I find that it helps me heal quite well and sooner than average. But it still took six years for the majority of it. And there are still little quirky things troubling me from time to time. But mostly I'm healed now.

And thank God the Health Department listened to me finally and shut the C.A.P.S. program down. Colorado doesn't need that old 1940s brick motel when they have 14 other newer and more sanitary facilities in the state.

My injuries and the ghosts weren't the only scary things there.

In December 2017 I had contracted some kind of "flu from hell" from that place just going on a tour, interviewing and filling out on boarding paperwork, pending my background check.

A week later I had spent 4 days in bed, thinking I was going to cough up a lung, and then suddenly it just stopped. Instantly.

But I returned to the facility to begin working there, and several residents ended up with the same type of infection, one even had to go on oxygen.

The scariest thing in that place was the uncleaned vents. What kinds of viruses were being incubated in there?

Yeah, I'm glad they shut it down.

Now it's getting renovated and flipped by some guy from New York, who stopped me as I was parked to go into the auto parts store next door, to ask me if I knew anything about any ghosts that were there.

I smiled.

"So those troubled souls are still there. Interesting," I mused. And then I told him everything I knew.

The Kind Yunweh Tsunsdi

Cece Perez, okay, because you asked I'll tell you. But this didn't happen on the REZ. It happened at my house in town.

So one morning a couple years ago, I had unexplainable insomnia. I wasn't stressed or anything. Just woke up about 2:30 am.

So I sat there playing a game on my phone hoping that would make me sleepy – lights off. Just playing with the light from my phone. And suddenly I heard a scritchy-scratch sound along the floor, coming from my laundry room and into the little alcove area between my bedroom door, the laundry door and the main part of the kitchen.

I glace up, and think I see my cat standing with her 3 lb self (on her hind legs) in front of my fridge in the kitchen and say, "Awwwww." Disappointed with the contents of my fridge. And weirdly wearing wooden stick armor (weird for a house cat) which is made of dogwood lashed together, sort of like bamboo armor in ancient Japan. The armor he or she was wearing had been dogwood, which means they are feeling friendly. If they wear ash wood it means they are angry.

I look back at my phone and then realize my cat is next to me on the bed, sleeping.

I look back over to that little spot in front of my fridge and this thing is gone.

Really cute face, dark brown and leathery. In fact, it's face was kind of like the porcupine that wandered into my yard out of nowhere a few days ago. Bipedal and standing about 2 feet high.

It's so funny to me that when I saw it I thought, "Oh, Yinyang," (My late cat's name,) instead of "What's that?"

And then right after it was gone, I became fully aware of everything that I saw. But it goes with what I was taught about them being able to teleport right through walls, and doing magic that includes mind spells. So honestly, it makes sense that the spell would evaporate off of me the minute the Yunweh Tsunsdi was gone.

132

So, I started leaving it treats with a little tiki-guy statue as a kind of way to signify this was for it to eat. It never ate any of the things I gave it. And the statue would always be turned backwards the next morning.

I start wondering if when I was singing The Morning Greeting to Grandfather Spirit and doing a few other things – because a few things is all I really know because of how I grew up – if this adorable little person followed me from Kentucky when we came back here to Colorado.

Kentucky is the original home quarters for the Tsalagi. Kentucky, parts of Tennessee, parts of the Carolinas. I think that's it.

Later I asked a tribal elder who said to plant wormwood and get two canines. But he's Paiute, not Tsalagi. Different experiences with the stick people by tribe. And he's the only one I can find anywhere near me of course, because this isn't Tsalagi territory.

I looked it up. There's this huge oval of area between my town and the backside of the Superstition Mountains where Ute and Paiute would be cautious while travelling because of the stick people they encountered in this area. They were not a friendly clan of little people, at least not then.

And then I remembered what I was taught when I was learning the old Tsalagi stories. Whisky and tobacco are their favorite gifts.

So now I leave whisky or tobacco whenever I gather herbs or sweet grass or rocks that I like. Especially if I see signs of their tiny homes.

I want to give a shout out to Marcus Cory who says he was taught to leave them candy. I think I want to try that sometime, too.

The Nice Mother-in-law

It was such a heartbreak that 6 months after my second ex-husband Carl and I got married, his very sweet mother died of cancer.

Out of his entire family that I met in the short 364 days we were together, she is the only person who made me feel welcome and accepted.

We took turns sitting with her at the hospital. I kissed her on her forehead after telling her to imagine a trip to Europe. A short time later she was gone.

And then came the funeral service at the funeral home in Baltimore.

Wouldn't you know it, her nasty sister, who had ripped all 6 of her kids away while they were young and got them scattered to different homes, had sent her daughter and her husband with a U-haul to load it up!

Ella Mae wasn't even in the ground yet, and not even a eulogy given!

These two vultures were not reckoning on me, with my little 5' 5" self getting in their way like a bull dog, but I did.

"This ain't nothing to you! You got no interest in this at all!" His cousin shouted at me in Ella's dining room.

"Oh, really?! Well look around you! All but one of Ella's daughters is here to say farewell, waiting quietly for the service time. And here's her son. Her only son! I'm his wife! You're only the niece! They all come first before you even get to look at anything, so I suggest you go back where you came from with that truck out there, and we'll let you know if there's anything left for you to have!" This whole time she was ducking behind her very tall husband as I walked them backwards to the hallway.

Then I started belly bumping her husband backwards down the hall and saying, "Get out! Go home! We'll call you later!" I did this until they opened the front door, went to the U-haul and left. Tires screeching. So funny.

His sister Georgia who was slightly mentally handicapped hugged me.

All Carl's sisters were surprised.

Ella's common law husband had looked up from his paper and had to chew back a laugh while it was happening, I had noticed this in the corner of my eye, but now he smiled and winked at me and then went back to reading his paper.

Ella Mae had assigned Georgia as her executrix, and had even written out a list on a little notebook for her to remember who was to get what. I was very stunned when I was given the buffet. Which I no longer have because I felt guilty keeping it after the divorce.

I was so sad that she had passed away. After a lifetime of never really being welcome in my family, here this woman had accepted me without a second thought. And now she was gone. I cried for days. And then I went and found a recipe for Koliva.

We held the memorial service at Saint Nicholas Greek Orthodox Church in Virginia Beach, Virginia, and I made the Koliva.

Father George said the blessings and called out the names of those being remembered that Sunday, and right as he had finished saying Ella's name, a gust of wind blew the sanctuary doors open - and there was a lobby with a second set of closed doors across from them that led to the parking lot! This was a powerful gust that made people's hair and clothes blow around. And it came from inside the building.

You should've seen the looks on people's faces that noticed me nodding at Ella Mae when she asked, "Is this all for me?" My heart welled up, and tears came to my eyes as we looked at each other and smiled. She was mistreated her whole life, just like me. We get each other, she and I.

Then she stepped back and sideways a couple of steps wearing her pink polyester pants and a white flowered top and holding a travel brochure!

Remember? I had told her while she was laying on the bed in the hospital it was okay to go now. And she could travel for free – imagine, Paris, Cairo, Rome? I was just being facetious and helping her let go with a little humor. Yet here she was with a travel brochure. That's just cool.

The weeks passed and I went back to college, since Carl wasn't keeping his promise to support me through Police Academy. This was how he got me to cancel in Salt Lake and move to Virginia with him and get married. But he lied.

He was okay with business college and becoming a paralegal, though. So that's what I did next.

One day, as I was brushing my hair and getting dressed in front of the long mirror in our bedroom I saw an old woman with another woman in her forties or fifties looking back at me over my shoulder. And they stayed there for a very long time. Even after I was finished dressing and brushing my hair they stayed there.

We looked in each other's eyes, and no words were spoken. I looked behind me, no one. Back in the mirror, there they still were.

I couldn't understand why they didn't at least show me something, because isn't that customary? When a ghost comes and stands behind you in the mirror, aren't they trying to convey a message? Don't they usually say something or think something at you?

Irregardless, I stayed there for several minutes. They both looked worried and I waited. And waited.

Finally, I asked out loud, "Is there something you need? Did you want to tell me something?"

Nothing.

And then they just sort of evaporated like shower steam.

I went and told my husband what I'd just seen. "Carl, I think the old woman was your mom here for a visit. But the younger woman I'm not sure about."

He whistled softly to himself. Then he smiled a mischievous smile.

"What?" I asked.

"You're something else. You just keep surprising me. I didn't know you could see ghosts."

"Carl, I told you that when the chapel doors burst open in a gust of wind during your mom's memorial service I saw her there. And that she asked, 'Is this all for me?' And I smiled at her and nodded."

"Oh, yeah. I forgot about that. The Koliva you made for her was good."

"I'm glad you liked it. But now I'm worried. What did she need me to do?"

"I wouldn't worry. Maybe she was just coming to say hello or goodbye."

I wrung my hands and went to gather my books for school.

I still feel like she was trying to show me something, maybe that younger woman?

I wonder.

Who was the younger woman?

The Stairs on State Street

I don't know why, but at this house that my cousins lived in, with the Clock Repair Shop on the front, the stairs figured into our games more than any other set of stairs. Leading our "prisoners" to the dungeon, going into a cave, and shooting the hot light bulbs with water guns so they'd break with a loud "POP!" were all in our repertoire at that place.

We are Gen-X, what can I say?

And while we are on about the stairs, shall we mention the spooky, poorly lit basement with way too many doors and not enough windows? Smelling of mothballs and sporting that 1960s black and white tile, but in a marble pattern instead of checks, there seemed to be extra people running around down there with us.

And hilarious to me, Aunt Carla and Uncle Lynn were as spooked by that basement as all of us kids were. The imposter parents mentioned feeling uncomfortable down there. Friends coming over to hang out said it was creepy.

And each of us had seen shadows looming where shadows shouldn't loom, right near a light that was on. And with 4 bedrooms down there, why did they all remain empty?

My cousin Jessie and her brothers and the aunt and uncle all crammed into the two upstairs bedrooms and the room that was supposed to be a dining room with a couple of bedsheets stapled over the arch for privacy.

Uncle Lynn would pretend to be too busy, and when he had anything he needed to put away down there, or to be retrieved, he would send one of the kids, who would always grab another kid to go with them. And then he and un-Alan would laugh nervously about the purpose of kids, so you don't have to deal with ghosts.

While we were staying with them, I don't think the imposter parents ever even ventured down into that area.

Aunt Carla would wait to put groceries and canning jars away in the pantry, until the kids were all down there playing. The same with doing laundry, because the washer and dryer were down there. It was like this unwritten rule, never be down there alone.

 The irony of 4 spare bedrooms and the large room that could've been a family room was always kind of funny to me.

When alone in that space, one could feel a strange, malicious anger at first.

But when I went down there alone a few times to get away from all the people, (8 kids and 4 adults are a lot of energy and noise and moods – even in a big house), the negative energy gradually subsided into a lonely sorrow and I could venture down the stairs and push the invisible force of turpitude into the corners, and relish the cooler air of the basement in summer, and the glazed, slick, smoothness of the thin mica tiles on my bare feet.

The smell of pinewood on the unfinished portions, nothing but studs fastened to the floor waiting for drywall, and the raw wood doors, were a comforting scent.

The darkness was more of dimness because some of the daylight gently tumbled into the basement windows and made silver sparkles out of the dust.

The noise of my family became almost silent.

Summer's sweltering heat vanished.

A mini-vacation.

But never would I ever go down there alone at night, because just like the way the daylight could tumble down into the windows and make the grey dust sparkle, so too could the night tumble down into the well of already inky emptiness, and I swear I saw shapes of men dressed in black doing creepy maneuvers into the rooms.

It made me wonder who got killed or if they all had been. And sometimes I would even see a male face bending in next to mine. Sneering at me.

This house was in Utah, and you already know how I feel about that place.

The Three Ghosts of Green Street

Across the street from our first apartment as a family in Craig, was the Lutheran Church on Green Street. And this residence had a trio of regular specters that liked to push my buttons.

Now said Lutheran Church used to be an Orthodox Jewish Temple, and I witnessed the very same with Orthodox Jewish families going in and out, up and down the double staircase one Saturday in 1981, when I visited this little town with my friend Andi (short for Andrea), whose father worked for the mines as a freelance geologist.

These people wore the typical Orthodox Jewish costume, women in wigs to cover their real hair, and a doily or hat over the wig. Skirts at least to just under the knee, preferably no higher than mid-calf in their traditions. Men and boys over 12 with their tzitzit hanging over their belts, tallit draped around their shoulders over their suit jackets, ringlets from their sideburns being grown to beard length and then curled. Boys wore a kippa, men wore a black hat.

I saw this. And this has been hidden and removed from the city archives. I even discussed this with Andi's mom, asking her specifically why they felt that this attire was required. She didn't know, she's not Jewish anyway. But the point is, it was there.

Not only this, but the Aharon used to sit between the blue stained glass windows on either side of it, and now a big ugly cross hangs there. I know this because I saw it online as it used to be when I was trying to find a new community to be a part of. I can't find it now. They're trying to disappear the Jews again.

I had been over there across the street pulling weeds from the tiered flower garden in the rain with the pastor's wife, and had been invited to services by her.

So I went, mostly out of a desire to create a network of friends. There were a couple of songs with a lot of Hallelujah in the chorus, and I sang it deep in my throat and with fervor. I love this type of songs.

The next afternoon, an acquaintance of mine came over to help me hang a coat rack on the wall in the little foyer to our tiny apartment across from said church, and then we just sort of clicked and spent several hours watching a movie, chatting inside, chatting outside. None of the conversations were really important, I think we were just craving human interaction, the two of us, and liked talking. (No, there was no sex, and anyway, my kids were there.)

As the day started to ebb from twilight into night, this new friend of mine invited me to go up to the cemetery and get scared in the dark up there. I told him no thanks, I see ghosts plenty, no need to go up there and see them all at once. It's draining.

He kept pressuring me, and suddenly we both heard this male voice shout, "Hey! Why don't you come over here and sing hallelujah?! You were over here yesterday singing hallelujah! Why don't you come over here right now and do it?!"

I looked at him, eyebrows raised and he almost made the same face. "Did you hear that?"

"Uh-huh."

"See what I mean? It's almost like I make it happen."

The male ghost kept repeating what he'd said in various ways. Then stopped after I shouted at him, "Hey, stop it."

My new friend decided he wasn't as interested in the cemetery as he'd formerly thought, and he probably should get home to his kids and make dinner.

I didn't argue. I had things to do myself.

That week I noticed the ghost of an old woman in one of those 1960s housecoats, the kind with the snaps down the front, who kept screaming at me to get out.

I kept telling her to shut up and then tried to ignore her. Finally I could take it no more.

"Get out?" I exclaimed. "You should get out. I don't see you doing any housework around here, nor do you bring any money into this household. You get out."

By the time we got to Friday and it was time to bring in the Sabbath with the three blessings, she had subdued herself and was at least tolerable. But after blessing the candles, the wine and the bread, this old man in suspenders, who had a pot belly and wore a ball cap grumbled, "Take your blessings out of here, we don't need your blessings."

"Oh, is that right old man? Well you can get out of my house then!" To which he turned and walked through the wall to the studio apartment next door.

I later told my friend Hila about this, and she asked me to describe the old man to her again. Her jaw dropped. Then she told me that the little studio apartment was where her father-in-law had lived until he'd died the previous year, 2010.

"Oh....so I was correct in telling him to get out of my home since he was living next door anyway."

She smiled and nodded. "He was a very cruel person when he was alive. I'm glad you told him off."

Now, of the 3 the most interesting one was the male who had shouted to us from the roof over the porch of the church. I had seen him there for a split second that night. He wore a layered haircut to his shoulders, had dark hair and was a little on the short side, and wore a taupe suit with caramel colored wingtips.

And I know all this because the 2nd time I saw him he was levitating in my foyer and I noticed as I stepped back from watering plants on the window sill.

All I could see was his wingtips and his shoes that time because the rest of him vanished up into the ceiling. What a weird way to manifest.

The third time I caught him waving to me through the front window to the right of the door and smiling.

These are the only ghosts I noticed at this little apartment, but I do believe that's plenty for such tight quarters.

The Yellow Ski Mask

I almost forgot to include the scary night when I was babysitting for the Aldens. They lived on the lower side of Thermopolis, and we lived at the top of the hill. I honestly can't remember for certain how I became their family's regular babysitter, I think he was one of Dad's bowling buddies or something.

I was so appreciated by them that they would hire me for most or all of the weekend, and I got a minimum of $5 each gig. Which means if I was babysitting Friday, Saturday and Sunday I would make an easy $15. If it went over a couple of hours they would pay me more. And for the average 13 year old in 1980, that was awesome.

Their house was a typical 1950s mock-up of a suburban home. Nothing but the basic rooms and sparsely furnished. The kids had minimalist collections of belongings, and so did the parents. So my signature hook where the parents return to a clean house and the kids are in bed was a breeze.

They didn't have cable, but the major 4 channels were able to be picked up by their little color box with rabbit ears, so all was good. UHF was in business by then and we could receive one of those in the town where I lived.

One particular weekend night after the kids were asleep, the only programming I could find on the boob tube was a horror flick wherein a babysitter is getting terrorized by a weirdo.

Right in the middle of the movie, there's a knock at the door. I freeze. Then I tell myself to pull myself out of the movie and see who it is.

I pull the little curtains back on the little window in the door and see a guy in a yellow ski mask who yells, "Boooogaaaaaloooogaaaaloooog!" Which, of course, scares the shit out of me and I felt my heart literally skip a beat as I dropped the corner of the curtain and flipped around to lean hard on the wall next to the door. And now I'm hyperventilating badly.

So I start trying to hold my breath like I do for the hiccups. If this is a real psycho, I need my strength back to protect myself and the kids.

And right then I recognized my obnoxious dad's laughter.

I open the curtain again and see him with his yellow ski mask rolled up like a cap and feel really stupid. I should've recognized the old raggedy thing. He'd had it forever.

I opened the door and asked him what he wanted, annoyed.

"The phone's disconnected and it's about an hour past the time the Alden's usually bring you home. Had to come check on you."

"By scaring me half to death, Dad?!"

He laughs again, leaning on his knees.

"Dad!!!"

"Sorry. It was just so good. Your eyes." He's still laughing, hence the short sentences.

"Dad, I was watching a scary movie! You made my heart stop!"

More laughing.

I just look at him.

He finally stops, stands up and asks me if I want a ride home.

"Dad?! No. These kids are all in elementary school. I have to stay until their parents get back."

"Okay. If it gets too much later, call me."

"Dad, their phone is disconnected."

"Oh, yeah."

"If anything happens, me and the kids already planned to run over to the neighbors across the street."

"Okay. But if this starts to be a regular thing, you probably shouldn't babysit for them anymore."

"Got it. Bye dad." I went in and shut the door.

But now the house was giving me the chills.

I started noticing the dingy 1950s pink paint in the bathroom, yellow in the kitchen, green in the living room. How everything looked like it had been prepared for a murder mystery movie.

And then I would hear these little noises in the kitchen, the bathroom, the parent's room. I kept getting up to look in the parent's bedroom, and of course nothing was there. But every time I looked in there, I got an image in my mind of this sad old lady with curly white hair and cat's eye glasses with rhinestones.

For some reason, the movie just wasn't as scary after that.

But the house was.

There's A Reason They Call It Water Street

As we moved into hurricane season the year after hurricane Katrina, I prayed and prayed that we wouldn't have a hurricane.

I got my wish, but we got one champion of a tropical storm.

I had not realized that Water Street could get flooded like that in Mobile, but it certainly can and did. We headed back on the loop of interstate 40 that descends into and rises from Water Street, coming back from temple services that afternoon, unaware until we were right in it.

The water was suddenly up to the middle of my door. And then the engine stalled. I was terrified.

There was a black pickup truck putting around helping people, nudging peoples back bumpers while they steered up to higher ground. Once there most of them had to call a tow truck because their engines wouldn't start again.

The guy driving it rolled down his window to holler, "Hey! Let me finish moving these folks over there and I'll be back to help you!"

Winded by too much adrenaline from the shock of it all, I just nodded back, smiled and waved.

But then I saw the water ripple across and move up almost an inch higher on some other people's car doors.

"Oh! Uh-uh!" I exclaimed. "Please, God, help me like you did during hurricane Floyd in Virginia, please, amen."

Then I tried starting the car. Nothing. So I asked the boys to climb out and help me push. As they opened their doors, water sloshed in, but not as much as I thought it might. And seeing a random little island of dry tarmac in the middle of it all, I told the boys, aim for there, I'll steer. Sha-sha got out and pushed from her side, I pushed from mine and the boys pushed from behind. We got her up there.

While we could then, I told the boys, "Hop back in here, close your doors, and I'm gonna try to start her up again."

I had to try about 3 or 4 times, but she finally roared to life. Then I used the belt like a little rudder thingy and revved and steered, revved and steered through the high water. There were a few shuddering instances where I thought we might stall out, but we kept going in that little Sonata, just like I'd been able to do in the Geo Metro a few years back.

I got us back to the house on Jackson Street, which was completely dry, and we all sat in the car listening to the forecaster to make sure it would remain safe there.

I said another quick prayer out loud, "Lord, I can't afford another car. If you help me keep this one running, I will make sure and give people rides who don't have cars as long as you let me know it's safe to do so."

Once I was confident we would be fine, I got out and walked to the nose of the Sonata and cleared debris from the grill, leaving the engine running. I did this because a male voice was murmuring in my ear to clean the manifold so the engine wouldn't die. "The manifold? What's the manifold?"

Now, I still am not confident that this cleaned the manifold, because I still don't know what that is for sure, but I was directed to clean that grill, so I did.

Then I heard instruction to clean the air intake, so I cleaned that area right under the windshield. Then I was told to lift the hood and get all the tree bits out of there.

My oldest, Ron-ron, was not going anywhere. As the oldest boy, he instinctively took leadership in situations like this, plus, I think he was curious. The other kids had gone inside and I asked Ron-ron if he wouldn't mind coming with me because I had just been told that we needed to keep driving the car until the white smoke went away so the exhaust system could dry out.

He was more than happy to be the important one. I think maybe his sister got way too much of the spotlight while they were growing up, but there's nothing I can do about that now.

We drove up and down all the main roads, but avoiding the wet ones. It took two hours to finally see the exhaust return to it's normal grey and whispy self. This put us at about 2200 hours after all was said and done.

I put the extra bath towels we had on the floor in the back of our little coupe, to soak up that water. It took two days to soak it all up, because a towel only has so much volume and there was a little extra water that kept running back and forth between front and back in the car.

The thing that confused me the most was how grey the water was, and how fishy it smelled. I used quite a bit of cleaning fluid, and even more air freshener in the cabin of that vehicle. More than I have ever used with any car.

It really baffles the mind when these things occur.

I don't know if the male instructing me was my gentleman ghost who called me Belle Israelle, or a different male spirit sent by the most high.

But what I will forever be grateful for is the fact that this vehicle served me well until we went back to California for a couple of years and then left it behind to move here.

I never forgot to give someone a ride when God pointed them out to me, and I never pulled over when he told me someone was a danger to me or my kids.

Yes, indeed. Water Street is named that for a reason.

Acknowledgements:

I'd like to use just one little page and take a moment to thank the particular employees at Paypal and Shutterstock and others who have my back. You know who you are. Thank you, again.

And all of the people who helped me remember things I should already know after using this type of software my whole life, but which for some reason I had to scavenge for in my own mind after a really bad concussion. Thanks for not making me feel dumb.

And to all the rest of you I might have forgotten at the Post Office, the Bank, and anywhere else I found the everyday kind of help all of us usually take for granted. Without it, I'd be even further behind the deadlines I set for myself.

About the Author:

Remedy Hawke has been writing in one genre or another since she learned how to write.

She loves writing in other languages as well, but only dabbles. Languages remind her of the codes she and her friends would create in school for play.

She loves languages and words so much, in fact, that her vocabulary assignments took all week to complete. And this is because she would be easily distracted by all of the other interesting words and their definitions along the way.

Her favorite classes in school and in college were any which required her to write creatively, seconded only by her love of gathering facts together.

She has several decades dedicated to utilizing these talents, both privately and professionally.

When she has had days off, she has clocked many hours of foreign films on streaming sites, and calls this "studying humanity". She collects foreign and ethnic cook books, poetry and novels by foreign authors and loves looking at period clothing and ancient architecture and art from various parts of the world. Music of almost every genre has played inside her four walls or on her car radio.

In her private time she has also been a member of various writers' guilds, and most enjoyed activities challenging members to write on a specific topic or from a list of words within a set time limit.

The she most adores biographies because of her love of people, and works of fiction – specifically science fiction and fantasy.

She has a few other works ready to publish soon, and hopes that by starting with this fun and frightening read taken from her own experiences, you will be able to get to know her sense of humor and her unique way of looking at the world.

One more thing. Reading this work might trigger a ghostly experience or two of your own. Feel free to record it below:

www.ingramcontent.com/pod-product-compliance
Lightning Source LLC
Chambersburg PA
CBHW071857020426
42331CB00010B/2556